Conversing with Dragons

Conversing with Dragons

A Celebration of Life and Art by Robyn Weiss

July 31, 1984–October 2, 2000

Compiled and edited by
Linda Joy Burke and Jacki Edens
with Introduction by Barbara DeCesare

iUniverse, Inc.
New York Lincoln Shanghai

Conversing with Dragons
A Celebration of Life and Art by Robyn Weiss

iUniverse, Inc.

For information address:
iUniverse, Inc.
2021 Pine Lake Road, Suite 100
Lincoln, NE 68512
www.iuniverse.com

Credit for photo of Robyn Weiss—David Terlizzi

ISBN: 0-595-28743-3 (pbk)
ISBN: 0-595-65844-X (cloth)

Printed in the United States of America

Conversing with Dragons is dedicated to Marguerite Morris, Bruce Smith, and all teachers who give freely of themselves as they support and nurture our children.

Contents

Contents

Introduction

The poems that Robyn Weiss wrote in the months before her death are important poems. They chronicle not just her battle with depression, but her love of the life she would later choose to leave. These are poems that are rooted in a very real world, but often they seek to reach beyond, into—as is the purpose of a poem—divinity. Art is the tool we use to build words that reach into infinity, the Divine. Robyn understood this and worked at it tirelessly.

When I read her manuscript for the first time, I was unprepared for the concrete images: the sap from a tapped maple, the houses and butterflies and rooms she shows us. I didn't expect mature observances from someone so young. Robyn is engaged in the world through these poems. In the clever parody of Poe, in her imagined banter at a men's shelter, and other narrative poems, we find her examining, critiquing, exploring the world, the people in it, and her relationship to it. We find her taking on characters in persona poems where she molds her voice into those of husbands, wives, laborers, and vagabonds. She resists the common urge of young writers to shut out the world and look only inward for voice.

As I read Robyn's work, I was reminded of the poems by John Keats. There is a similarity in each writer's use of art to heal, to soothe. Both writers, confronted with their mortality, challenged it in verse. They attempted to come to terms with the frailties of the body and of the world. Robyn wonders about her ability to shed anger and depression in "Another Season of Sugaring," likening the successes when she writes:

and I wonder
how much
boiling down I must do
to reach
my own
sweet essence?

Along with Keats, there are flashes of Plath, of Sappho, there are mythological and literary references throughout. Robyn certainly anticipated her work would join the voices ever reaching into the sacred space that art aspires to.

We readers have from Robyn this collection of poems that promise. We can only imagine how her craft would have unfolded for her, blossoming with experience, learning and teaching life's lessons on her pages. It is the unfortunate bedfellow art finds in sorrow, but Robyn is neither the first nor the last whose art outlives her. Our literary community is lucky to have had Robyn join in the ancient efforts to speak into infinity, and Robyn must know her voice is heard. Her writing is, quite literally, her life's work. Her words co-mingled now with infinity.

Barbara DeCesare

Thoughts from the Editor

I want to tell you about Robyn Weiss, a gifted poet and writer who joined the Baltimore Writers' Alliance in August 2000 as an intern on one of the organization's publications *The Baltimore Review.* We met in July at the Columbia Festival of the Arts "In Love With Words" Poetry Day. You see, I had been the judge for a Howard County Library sponsored School Poetry contest in which Robyn was a prize winning contestant. I remember conspicuously slipping out of the world-renowned poet Edward Hirch's keynote that morning, so that I would be in time to hear the winners of the middle and high school contests read in another room at the festival.

I stood in the back and listened to Robyn read the poem which had received an honorable mention along with a few other poems she had written. I was impressed. In a discussion at the reading, some of the students lamented that the teaching of poetry and, more importantly, students' poems were not taken seriously in area high schools. When Robyn read her poems though, it was clear that someone was taking her seriously. She told me later that hers were some of the few poems her teachers enjoyed reading.

John Constantini[1], one of her teachers at Centennial High School, says "she would have made the 19th century poet Alfred Lord Tennyson proud." Even though she was only sixteen, she had completed two novels and was working on her third, had written several short stories (one of which was awarded a Balticon[2] prize posthumously), and over 150 poems which she had stored on her computer.

We wound up hanging out together at the festival, not because she had seen me read. She hadn't. We hung out because I saw her read. I thought she was an

---

1. Columbia Flier 10/12/2000—Jennifer Vick
2. Maryland's Regional Science Fiction and Fantasy Convention presented by The Baltimore Science Fiction Society

interesting, quirky, intelligent child with a passion for writing. She was also stuck with knowing she was an oddity in a world where the things she thought about were incomprehensible to her peers. Because of what I saw in her, I suggested that she come to work with the BWA. She enthusiastically accepted my invitation and in late August began working as an intern with *The Baltimore Review*.

On Monday October 2nd, according to an article in the October 12th edition of the Columbia Flier, "Weiss walked off the top of a parking garage." I found out by reading an email from her mother, which at first left me suspended in disbelief. I really thought it was a prank, and I rushed off to the funeral home down the street where the viewing was scheduled. There I met one of the funeral directors, a kind, sturdy woman, who knew the pain of losing a child herself. She answered my worried questions, and told me that the family would really appreciate it if I came back for the viewing.

When I returned to see Robyn, she lay there perfect in her death surrounded by some of her favorite belongings. Her mom told me, "Now I understand why she liked Pyramids. You can bring everything with you when you pass on. I want to put her whole room with her." I fumbled with words, which I knew could never be enough. I told her how talented her child had been, knowing I was probably telling her something she already knew. I didn't find out until I read the Columbia Flier article how troubled she had been, apparently most of her life. I didn't know because in the Summer of 2000 she had been doing well and was happily doing the thing she loved—writing.

I'm the kind of person who looks for the lessons in every moment. In this moment I found myself once again confronted with the awful randomness of death juxtaposed with the immediacy of a life lived with obvious passion. I have been reminded how important it is to live and love, as Marge Piercy says, "concretely, consciously, and conscientiously."[3] I believe that was what Robyn, with all her amazing imagination, wanted to do too. I also take to heart Rabbi Grossman's words (from Anna Olswanger's interview with him in the September 2000 issue of *Wordhouse*) when he declared that "writers can correct the world." In Robyn, I saw one writer doing her best to do just that. Unfortunately for her, it was not enough.[4]

---

3. "To Have Without Holding"—from *The Moon is Always Female* by Marge Piercy

4. "Remembering Robyn Weiss"—first printed in *Wordhouse: Newsletter of the Baltimore Writers' Alliance*—November 2000

A memorial scholarship fund in Robyn's name has been set up for students who show promise in writing. All monies from the sale of this book will go into this fund.

Linda Joy Burke

Robyn

Singer, poet, reader, daydreamer
Friend of gryphons, unicorns, dragons
Who feels enthusiastic, highly opinionated, slightly bored
Who needs understanding, intellectual stimulation, time to think
Who gives love, a sympathetic ear, unwanted advice
Who fears slugs, pain, death
Who would like to see the whole world, true love, heaven
Who knows how to ride a pegasus, reason with a troll, converse with
dragons.

Portraits

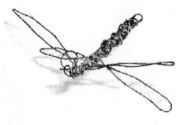

August 24, 2000

Dear Mommom and Papa,

This is a letter from your Grand-Daughter. I have decided to name Myself the Goddess of Literature (move over muse Cleo). Henceforth, I shall refer to Myself in capital letters, as befits a powerful Deity.

How are things back in the old country? We are doing pretty well up here, though Lara and I are more than a bit sorry that school is starting again on Monday. Where did the summer go? I was so busy for the most part that time really flew by; it has only been in the past couple of weeks that it felt like summer should. You know, the long, lazy days that you feel like doing absolutely nothing. Come to think of it, I feel that way most of the time. Each to Her own, I suppose.

I am writing to you from Mom's computer because Mine is in the shop getting repaired, though We can't seem to figure out what is wrong with it, it just won't turn on. The laptop is perhaps the best aid that I could get to further My writing. My only regret is that I had not backed everything up for over a week when it stopped working, so I hope that it can be fixed without losing My data.

Though I am sorry that summer is over, I am quite enthusiastic about My classes for this year. The schedule is somewhat daunting; all academic subjects. Due to some odd goings-on, I have replaced My singing group (they didn't appreciate Me anyway—the ingrates) with the school newspaper, and what was Spanish is now Native American History with the wonderful Mr. Smith. My math, English, and social studies classes should prove very challenging. The American History teacher is an incredible man; he was a Rhodes Scholar (like Our dear Mr. Clinton), has his doctorate, and is published. I can't wait to be in his class.

End of update. You may go back to worshiping Me.

Robyn
Deity of Literature
Master of the Written Word
Final Author-ity
Editor of Ambrosia
Universe-Famous Poet Laureate
Intern at the Baltimore Review

If You Come Knocking

Daughter sleeping,
wife soaking in tub,
I sip one more glass of wine.
Read Zen poems of Ryokan.
Outside, the night sky darkens,
Venus sets low in the west.
If you come knocking at my door,
be prepared to sit in silence.

Another Season of Sugaring

Ten years in a row
drilling holes
hanging jugs
gathering sap
building fire
boiling down
at this turn
of the season
snow drifts in woods
woodcock in dusky sky
this final boiling
as I feed dry maple
into fire pit
under old roasting pans
roiling away
steam ascending upward
as I reach down
for dessert wine
kept in snow bank
and maple ice
sweet coolness
as hot sap
evaporates into
nearly dark sky
and I wonder
how much
boiling down must I do
to reach
my own
sweet essence?

Namesake

The fire of my youth
Consumed old timber
Leaving ember unconscious
And gray ash upon my scalp.
As my namesake,
I came from the woods,
With their faces turned within shadow,
Away from illuminated fields.
The universe I knew as a child
Went on forever in darknesses
Beyond my ken.
The stars, we know,
Are short of destiny
And this smoldering earth
Would burn to the last tree
And the sun dance on her bones to the lyre.
The Truth is vaster
Than me or the forest.
What I imagine is part of
Playing what I know,
What I think I know,
What I suspect I believe.
We grope and shoot forward
So that beyond stars
We may become what we are.

The Visit

Clouds in the sky
Tossed like kites
Visiting the graves
Forgetting just why
They all came to day
Flowers are placed
Leaves raked away
Love was misplaced
Brought back for a day
Then tucked away
Until next year.

When I was a child, I would go to the cemetery with my grandparents.
We would clean each of the family plots, rake away the leaves,
Fill the urns with flowering plants.
Our fallen warriors received a new cloth flag.

After my grandfather died, my grandmother hired an Irish bagpiper to come with
us while we were erasing the debris left by winter, the piper would play.

I am eighteen hundred miles from the place,
where my family is buried.
Who cleans the graves in the spring?
Who plants the flowers?
Who lovingly sets out the flags?

No one is left to care or prepare.
No one is there to call for the piper
No one to care for the graves.

I hear the echo of the piper
and my heart aches.

Who will be there for me?

Story to Be Told

Houses, rows upon rows,
There is a story to be told,
A sadness, like a cancer, grows,
Smiling faces turn ever so cold
As they stare out the blind fold.

Barren trees, row upon row,
There is a story to be told,
A cut deeper than the truest arrow,
Beauty becomes a commodity to be sold,
Scarring the land for pieces of gold.

Soldiers, rows upon rows,
There is a story to be told,
Marching now against their foes,
They break the warrior's mold
Crossing over Death's threshold.

Tombstones, row upon row,
Of the everyday young and old,
Like some forgotten fellow,
Who was neither timid nor bold,
But whose life will never be told.

Armada

The wind still drives us. Fate and the kiss of distant gods.
But we have seen the first phonic annunciations of day
and we make our way into the slipstream of life, the odds
still unbeatable, but we are resolute rogues in this way:
We give over the tiller to no other. For in a universe where God
does not deny us the choice of roads, what right has flesh
or mortal agency to lay the buoys and chart the wheel
and say to us in voices ripe with a coward's bullying that we can
do nothing but what they would have us do? For do we not feel
what we alone can feel and chart what we alone can plan
and kiss with eyes open or closed of our own volition?
Beyond the limitations of the form and aspect of our fate
we are the caretakers of a history yet unwritten, our position
in the constellations that future generations shall navigate
by is yet plastic to the touch. We have our Creator's permission
to sail to the edge of the world or to sew sails for those who dare to.
We have our Creator's blessings to make of life a feast or a funeral.
You have the inalienable option to dream mighty dreams, if you care to,
and to swear in a tongue alien to all but you and God that you will fall
not to the night, for the morning is upon us, and we are born, anew.

Bridge Across the Harbor

She straddles the narrows like a lean young lover,
Preparing for the evening of repose.
Her only adornment, a long necklace
Strung with twinkling diamonds and rubies,
Set against a purple night sky.
Across the bay, over her shoulder,
The Lady in the Harbor peers into the thickening darkness,
Torch held high as if to expose to the world
The shameless spectacle at the very entrance to
The greatest City in the world.
She stares resolutely, indignantly
At the wanton hussy, long slender legs
Spread in open invitation to all, large and small,
To freely pass in and out through her nubile limbs,
Seemingly oblivious to the glare of the mighty Goddess of Liberty.

Hobo Ken; Vietnam Vet

Packaged with torn, dirt stained,
blue jeans stitched to his waist,
an old, green army jacket covering his plastic chest.
A brown beanie molded on top his head,
he didn't come with a sword or gun,
but a tin cup to collect change from strangers.

Again, the Soldier

War held no comfort for me
And still I find no peace
For my body aches with the constant memory
Of the death that overtook me…

My body burns with metal thorns
And I fall beneath the splintered trees
Of the once mighty country.
And as my mind is cleared by death
The screaming is silenced
And the pain is eased
And the shackles of pride are broken at last.
I shout to the men around me
Why do you fight this war?
Who is it you guard?
But I see their minds are closed to reason
And their eyes closed to shame.
An explosion
And I am covered with the blood-soaked earth.
I have died in vain.

Urban Angel

She wore black boots and gray skies
on that first Sunday I met her
and cried tears that washed the cigarette ashes
off the side of my car.
Carved into her palms
were strange sunflower stigmata
she said appeared overnight
after reading Ginsberg's sunflower sutra
for the first time at 15.
She was 18 and fresh
and she wandered the streets
of this fascinating gizmo city at midnight
looking for fellow hipsters and acid jazz freaks
to recite poetry with over cups of steaming loneliness.
Her soul had been lost in the suburbs somewhere,
but she'd given up her search of coffee shop
and beat joint lost and found boxes,
cultivating now the poems of Ferlinghetti and Rimbaud
in her guts in place of it.
At night she wrapped herself in sunsets
of smog and solitude
and pursued the only honest life she knew.
She had Miles Davis and Charlie Parker heroes
and she could fly on the wings
of rapid fire Castaneda crows,
but her dreams were grainy-textured noir-fests.
She had no screen idols.
There was no perfect absolution
for her abstract life
as she lived within the seams and cracks of the city.
I encountered her again years later,
picked her up hitchhiking to Omaha.
We rode together in silence
along highways of darkness and illuminated exit ramps
until the soulful music of B.B. King,
that played like voices in her head,

moved her to speak about her father
and how she couldn't recall his face,
of the first man she'd ever held naked in her arms
and how she could still feel his delicious lips
on her body,
how Dylan Thomas left her feeling vulnerable,
so she hated him,
how R.E.M. had kept her alive
during the one winter she was depressed and fetal,
though she'd never listened to them since,
how she loved the smell of a wool sweater,
damp with the first mist of fall,
and then we parted.
I went on to New York
and I'll never know
what drew her with totemic urgency to Omaha
but I loved her then,
I know that;
though I never knew her name.

At the Mission

It was just another day at the mission.
The bums, smelling like the seats of their pants
Were stacked like a roll of wooden nickels
Under a sky with mixed feelings.

Duecy was tryin to sell Detour last week's Time
Sayin it was a girly mag,
When the sound of a distant siren
Made all heads
Rise
And
Fall
Like somebody dropped the name Jeeeesus in a convent.

Old dirty-headed Charley moved his whiskered jaws
To grind long-forgotten teeth,
Sputterin out tobacco,
Eyes winkin on and off
Like lights at a train crossin
Warnin of oncomin words,

"Down the Baptis' mission ya gotta pray ta eat."
He rubbed his sooty head and winked even harder
"De Catlicks, dey jus' feed yas."

Just then,
Welfare Mike,
Thumblock on the business end of a
Canadian Ace "Jug-o-Beer"
Hit the line roarin out a sea chanty.
He was nine sheets
With elbows sharp as broken glass
When he exploded into a hornpipe
Scatterin the boys like fish on a deck.

Some went down like bowlin pins
And some like broken birds,

Their curses,
Rusty as death rattles,
Rising on small puffs of bad breath.
Some shook themselves up with anger.
Others stayed down,
And shook like the insides of broken clocks.

Mike,
He kept movin,
The impersonation of a drunk.
Eyes rolling
Mouth writhing,
He wrestled out words in Portuguese,
Every now and then
Holdin up his hands
For close attention
To a line that held great meaning.

All the boys were singin and cheerin along
By the time Fat Father Freddie
Popped like a pimple
From the doors of St. Louis,
His head, a road map of blood vessels
Bursting above his cassock.
All eyes turned churchward,
And to the sign,
"No man will be served who has been drinking liquor."
A man of black cloth
And red skin,
Lou Costello in a skirt,
Father Fred descended on Mike
Fists flailing
Flutter punches
And Stinky ("I'll HURT YOU!") kicks,
Till Mike hit the gutter
Singing a different tune.

From the heights of the church
The stone faces of the saint's crusade
Looked on with the gargoyles.

Translation

We will obtain lab work
(puncture the skin)
(taking my blood)

Valium will be given
(please notify of any allergies)
(I am in a false state of euphoria)

An ultrasound will be performed
(the echo of heartbeats)
(I have no heart)

Talking to the nurse will help you feel
(more at ease)
(I really love your shoes. Do you run?)

Xylocaine will be administered. This is the numbing
(medication.) (I am already numb)

Blunted sterile rods will be used to dilate…(papa can you hear me?)
and will cause minor cramping (papa can you see me?)

We will suction out the contents
(do not panic) (I am sorry, sorry, sorry)

You will be able to walk to the recovery room and relax
(I cannot relax in these shoes)

Ghost Parade

Sonya calls
wanting sex and punishment at 4am
laughs nervously
fearing rejection
knows her looks are quickly leaving her at 42
and climbing.

Rosie rings at 6pm
asks for companionship
short-lived romance and multiple orgasms
fearing a jealous husband
she grasps for love on pale unicorns.

Dawn is still a teenager at 32
rebels against parental golden rule
stealing quick oral interludes
behind her fiancé's back
aching for serene afternoons
when sweet and dreaming at 16.

Maria runs away
a year and a half
left her hating the ready-made family
caring little for broken hearts
promises lying shattered
as glass on the kitchen tile.

Alisa gave up long ago
abused by uncles and self-hate
continues to ruin father, son and daughter relations
denying a childhood for her kids
she churns out mistake No. 4
another baby on the way to a similar fight for attention.

Ghosts
all of them
parading empty halls
in a house of fleeting hopes
spilled on the floor and left
to stain the rug.

Waiting to Begin

This is the modern Galilee
Herod runs with Roman backing
Samaritan man, waiting to begin
Among the Gaelic Pharisees

All aboard the Mind-ship *Calcified*!
Mind your step, your head, your questions
Set your sail in all directions
Due to depart on some evening's tide

Life is painful without living
Nothing gained through endless thought
Something lost by aimless drought
Seas make no waves without stirring

With passing age, this becomes sin
I am standing on well-known shores
Looking for unfamiliar stars
Judean Celt, trying to begin

And though the New World carries fear
It far surpasses no surprises
Grandly dwarfs the enterprises
Of the Old World carrying bare

Madness

Myths

"*The Mythology Times*," I read aloud, looking over Mom's shoulder at the computer screen. "Interesting. Was that a school project of Lara's?"

"Probably," she replied, already thinking about something else. She has a fast mind, my mother does; never expending energy on something old when there is something new to think about. My younger sister Lara is like that also; never expect her to still be thinking about the same thing ten minutes later, unless, of course, it's homework. She clings tenaciously to homework like a barnacle to the hull of our sailboat. I wish that I could say the same thing about myself, but I tend to get distracted by other things. This also applies to my own "projects"; I have many partially written stories, often just the introduction, though sometimes several pages long, and two half-finished novels. I tend to get really excited about a new idea, work on it for a day or two, or even a week, before I get bored with it or stuck on a certain part and I wander off to something more interesting or less difficult. Right now, I am "officially" working on an adaptation of Mozart's *The Magic Flute*, typing up "Songs of Middle Earth" which is a compilation of all the poems in J. R. R. Tolkein's *Lord of the Rings*, trilogy, as well as a poem or two. Somehow, *The Mythology Times* seemed like a great idea; I would write humorous accounts of the ancient myths telling what was going on "currently" with all of the old gods. I ran down the steps, racing for my beloved companion of my lonely days of writing, my five-year old Aptiva. Dear little thing, it has stuck with me through thick and thin and everything else in between. I sort of get the feeling that it is only happy when I sit and converse with it and I am convinced that it gets lonely when I am away.

Anyway, back to reality, I raced down the stairs, but was interrupted half-way down by my mother yelling, "Take a shower!"

I protested feebly, but to no avail. Poor women, she doesn't seem to understand that personal hygiene takes a weak second place to creative inspiration. Whilst showering, the true élan of the idea was fled to greener and dryer pastures. I felt like Samuel Taylor Coleridge when someone interrupted him in the midst of writing "Kubla Khan" and what was perhaps the greatest poem in British history was lost to us for all time. Ah, well, all hope was not gone; I forgot the method that I planned to use for writing *The Times* but I did end up with a nice little piece of the same title, which chronicles the not-writing of *The Times* from that moment of divine inspiration until it was not set down on paper to become what was not my best piece of work yet. Perhaps you will read it someday.—

Sisyphus

Eternal damnation is not always obvious.
Anyone who reads the myth of Sisyphus must wonder
What kept him eternally straining against his rock;
A logical man would just walk away
And never return to the cursed hill.
It isn't what you'd think.
No-one blocks the exit.
And no-one is there to stop him if he just sat down.
Not Cerberus bearing ghastly fangs,
Nor the Furies with their fiery whips,
Nor Hades himself, Dark Lord of Death.
No, what keeps Sisyphus pushing his boulder,
And trudging back down to brace and shove it again,
Even after decades, centuries, millennia,
Is the thought that, that last time,
It looked like he was finally getting somewhere.

Dawn Prophecy

Mirrored waves of liquid dreams solidify as crystal streams,
while far beyond the moonlit beams illuminate the writhing sea.
Beyond the simple way of thought, where men ne'r dare to join the lot
of sacred symbols finely wrought, consuming mortal imagery.

Enshrouded in a veil of fear, the ivy covered stones appear
to breathe with life and shed a tear for those who wandered off the path.
Within, behold a wealth of old, chandeliers adorned in gold,
and tapestries of silken mold, secure beneath the gates of faith.

Before the age when time was young, before the pharaohs myth was sung,
when ancient fathers' mystic tongue spoke silent of the newborn bane.
Amongst the creatures of the night it arose aloft, as dragons might,
and in its path of wave of blight did blanket as torrential rain.

Beware the setting sphere, they say, for darkness cannot hide the prey,
and one by one his victims lay, without a prayer and half-alive.
The quest to find the answers to a hopeful question no one knew,
yet no one suffers as the few, who perish not, yet can't survive.

Mind Whirls

The tide, the tide
Swishing me, dragging me
Down, down…cold!

Black ink swirls around me,
Staining my clothes, my body,
Cocooning me in thick, oppressive air.

Where's the illuminated Passage which will guide me onwards?
There is nothing but a gradual un-darkening ink,
Fading up to depressing gray mist and three paths.
I travel up to the gates of Heaven,
Where gleaming white marble and golden gates await.
A whispering wind focuses its path upon me.
I whirl in it, seeing the gilt of Heaven,
the charcoal-dusted, blood-stained gate of Hell,
And catching glimpses of that wild, tangled, forested fairy Path.
And beyond, the River of blood that Thomas rode through.

"Go," the zephyr moans.
"You are not for here,
lose yourself amidst the mist."

I go, stumbling into that which has claimed
The memories of ancient mariners.

I turn to a sky, deep blue.
The desert sun ripples
With the heat of my
Icy heart.

The multi-winged trees fly haphazardly in my mind.
I can't watch the collision of swans and elephants.
Dementia in the form of a flying waxed moustache
Celebrates my confusion with melting clocks,
Marking my eternal last moments.

"Tick, glop"

The melted seconds fall into my hands,
Quicksilver,
Mercury,
Slipping through the cracks in my fingers.

Slipping,
Falling,
Puddling
Silver on my life-stained sneakers,
To slip into the thirsty, yellow sand

Run away little boy,
Stay not in the labyrinth's sweet embrace.
Stay not to see angels' tortured by Helen's face.
Stay not to see,
For to see is to love,
To love is to care.
Don't blow your horn,
Elvis was never in the building.

Dreams

The dreams of gods are bittersweet;
their mead,
unknown by mortal man.
With lofty thoughts,
they view the naught—
and ponder eon's brooding span.
Come ye, to this,
the elder gate—
the house of dragon's ancient clime;
come dream the dream,
that others deem,
that steeps of rust,
and drips of time.
The gods, they stretch,
and shake the Earth,
they did this at creation's birth.
With piercing eyes,
they seek the prize,
and hold from all
their raucous mirth.
What is their joy,
you dare to ask,
what is this ancient, lofty task?
But yet you know,
when gales do blow,
the mystery drowns you in its flask.
Come ye, and ride the wings of dawn,
when all was naught,
and all was gone;
the dreams of men,
they weave and spin,
but dreams of gods,
they linger on.

Father Phoenix

The day begins to warm
Cold patches of mud
Once scorched barren from its presence
An old man sits watching
Time slowly choking away remnants of his life
Cries of a newborn
Echo as they bounce from nursery walls
Surrounding it like love

But, oh, father phoenix,
Sister sun,
Draw me in and
Push me out,
Passing through clouds of darkness,
Blessing shields of light.
Everything between
There after and again
Father phoenix
Sister sun
Everything into one

Rain falls
From yesterday's clouds
Last week's puddles
It charges down
The sequoia that stumbles
The one who falters
Are resurrected
Basking in light of the new day
The universe in our hands changes
Falling and ebbing like the tide
A thousand acres
Into a thousand lives
Father phoenix
Sister sun
Everything into one

Journey Back to Ithaca

In your paintings there is always a lone figure—
sometimes human, sometimes bird—lurking
in the darks of your canvas, edges illuminated

by some unknown light source. Perhaps the moon?
When I visited your studio, there you were:
amid all your monoprints and easels,

stacks of murky blues and muddy browns,
the sun lighting your body from behind;
Ulysses in the art colony, riding your horse

gracefully through the shades. Your Ulysses
rides with a tired, but arrogant, posture,
his shirt sleeves rolled up and his chin slack.

The horse leans too, still keeping its rider up,
but thirsty and long-ready to stop and nap.
There is no safe place to lie down, though:

The pale-eyed master shakes his graying head,
so they continue on. A flash of lightening follows
them across a darkening shadow of sky.

The Thinker

Transfixed in meditative silence
With bended arm upon bended knee
What Promethean thoughts burn within your mind?
How the Supreme Consciousness brought forth the pendant world from the void
Or how with one taste of that outlawed rind
Death's black maw opened upon mankind
And corruption was made the mortal legacy?

Perhaps vibrant stars you so consider,
The body cosmos, the measureless shroud of space
Unspoken worlds that never basked in the heat of a sun
Or is your tooled skull a mundane thing?
Debating the proper length of a hair or the angle of a smile
Aching to understand a love that passes understanding
Frozen by Medusan vanity in an eternal pine

Or have I misjudged you still, my quiet foe?
Do you mock me with your perpetual brood?
A Puckish aping of meditative man
Biding time whilst it bides us
So moved to contemplate the contemplator contemplating
Transfixed in meditative silence.

Lexis

Musings

The poetry muse who inspires is relentless.
She demands, besieges, implores,
Then whimsically deludes.

The inspirational nymph purrs a word,
A word that challenges, dares for more.

She slides onto the pages of books,
Giving just one phrase, an image.
I stop, story interrupted, plot interfered,
One word given gives birth to more.

My muse meanders, winds her way through songs,
Forget the melody, the rhythm, the composition.
Waiting, lingering, whispering her messages;
Her voice inspires.

A rendezvous to connect,
Anytime, anywhere.
Haunting movies, magazines,
Maneuvering words, guiding
Until I have paper under my pen.

Mathematics Courts Literature

Literature appeared, leaving her castle of words, trailing silver metaphors.
Moonlight touched her face, luring her into a poetic garden.
She paused to think, resting beside a river of flowing ideas.
Suddenly, she heard a steady footstep through the flowering shrubs.
Fearful, lest the person see her beauty rare, she enveloped herself in a cloak of ambiguities.
Mathematics approached—tall, slender, with an exactness that made her tremble.
He spoke: "Oh, mistress of language, why must you hide your elegant beauty? I beseech you—glance at me".
Literature coyly smiled and seemed to laugh beneath the protective cloak.
"I have many suitors. I am courted by Linguistics. What can you offer me?"
"I have manifold destinies, singular points, vector fields of thriving grain,
Coordinate rings of ruby and diamond. All these I offer you."
He kissed her cheek,
She blushed and turned away.
"You are too bold, sir."
"It is my way to come to a swift conclusion."
They embraced in a shadowy corner of infinite space.
And the galaxies winked to see the pair linked
As they rode a nebula of possibilities—

Alone in the Lit. House

I sit in this chair,
Alone, in the lit. house,
As I type on the laptop
I got for my birthday
Two months before,
I look up at the walls
And wonder how alone I am
With poets and writers
From all over the place
Watching me
From silent photographs
Adorning these old halls.

Maya Angelou's motherly concern,
e. e. cummings's uneasy stare,
Nathaniel Hawthorne, arrogant, as usual,
James Fenimore Cooper, placidly ignoring,
Gertrude Stein's stony gaze,
Mark Twain's bushy intolerance,
Edger Allen Poe, tortured, of course,
D. H. Laurence bares his teeth,
Allen Ginsberg, owl-like,
William Shakespeare's enigmatic smile.

They gaze down,
Unperturbed
By my intrusion
At this late hour
Of the night.

Book

Four walls, a door, a window closed,
A bed, a chair, a book of prose.
And as he slowly scans the lines,
A light from deep within him shines,
For he sees not, this dingy room,
He sees a land where flowers bloom.
A land where time and tide stand still,
Where all is ruled by nature's will.
For he is lost amongst the pages,
Away in far off distant places.
When he returns, awakes, to see,
This bitter stark reality,
He'll feel not pain nor dark despair,
He'll see the book before him there
And know that he still holds the key
To unlock this cage and become free.

On Wings of Words

When rich with folded solitude,
Beyond the fettered drone of pain,
I view a span of topaz jewel
Above the earth, beneath my hand;

Where up the sacred sun alights
With blazing beams that sear my gaze,
And boasting of its fiery might
Begets the dazzled blue its rays.

Below, through lazy scallop domes,
A creature breaks the open air;
And gives its spanning wings alone
To starlight ringing absent there.

It rides the wake of Heaven's rim
Aloft where watchful angels fly;
Its beauty but a floating whim
Beshadowed in the living sky;

It flies a whispered fantasy
That ever dwells, beyond my touch,
With blinding dreams my eyes would paint
If but my mind could hold a brush.

In the Lee

What would I say if I had the words?
Why should I say anything at all?
If through non-action everything is done,
Through silence that all is spoken?

What would I say if I had the words?
I dream in the wonders of music and verse
Yet daylight hours condemn me to prose.
Is music only a waking dream?

What would I say if I had the words?
Would I tell you I loved you and find it true?
Does making it verbal make it real?
Should I say nothing to bind you less?

What would I say if I had the words?
Would I tell of laughter and song?
Or would I spill woe all day long?
Perhaps silence is best,
So now that words are not allowed,
I find I need them more than ever.
Life flows onward,
Me in the lee;
And I, I say nothing—

Metaphorically Speaking

Dead metaphors stalk the tender prose
Squeak and gibber in the rows
Among the dark and dank and empty words
When writer's mind is taken unaware,

Enchanted by the ebb and flow
Of the rhythm that you know
Will have you nodding, nearly napping
Suddenly they're everywhere they're not supposed to be.

They're not really dead, you know
Like Brer Fox, they're lying low,
Waiting for a little lapse
To rob your words of life, like vampires in the night.

Not the dawn's early light
Gives these goblins any fright
"Delete this," they quaver
And suck the marrow from your words.

Dead metaphors will not be stilled
Won't stay buried nor fresh ones willed.
So listen for the still, small voice,
And beware of eager volunteers.

Of My Muse

She senses me cool in the eve's delight,
softly wraps me in the lamb's wool of my blood.
And I crave her fiercely deep in night
if I ignored her rustling skirts
near evening time.
She would shroud my soul in desire's design,
knowing of hatred. And lusting. And you;
so I felt sugar-sticky kisses wetting my skin.
She left me long before the dawn—

To know her borders on sanity's balcony,
towards seeing all man's putrid thoughts
from windows far above the merriment.
To her I must go, alone,
naked in the malty spring air.
To know her is to know the icy polar ends,
head and toes in blistering ice.
And she keeps my middle warm.

Every poet's dreams are kept in her heart,
hopelessly lost in the throes
of her cannibal passion.
And the slaughter houses slew blindly.
And the daytime was only corrupted confusion.
And the night offered no solace. Only darkness.
She took this mortal passion. Gone.
She will fill my heart if I love her. Madly.
She will grant me to suckle her sweet. Disease.

What to do if she leaves me lonely?
I'll seek the sweetness in passion
as honey and fire.
The woods are thick, the animals treacherous,
yet we're already stumbling
down her path.

David

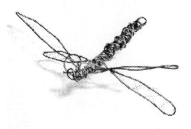

Shepherd's Song: Job Interview

My boss is going completely mad,
but then, that is why I was hired:
to play the strings of my kinnar-harp
to sound a balmy air for the tempest
of his fear, to calm his ravaged nerves.

I must commute a twelve-mile walk
between his house (Gilgal of Saul)
and my father's flocks which wander
over rocky soil
in the craggy Hills of Judea.

When I'm with the sheep, I compose
music to soothe the savage king,
the anointed of God—who, because
he did not follow precise orders in the battle
against the Amalekites, was rejected by God—

but when I'm with Saul, I think of battle,
sharpening spears, taming the voices he hears,
longing for peace and shepherding.
I think of the lion, whose step I hear among
the rocks, and how my heart dances at the sight

of his mane. I see him steal along the crags,
eyeing my lambs for his dinner—waiting, muscles
quiet but ready, for attack. We wait alike.
Meanwhile, I play my kinnar so the sheep
will not remember that they can smell fear.

When he trots beside the sheep, mane trailing,
picking up graceful speed, eyes trained on food—
my sheep—the strumming stops. I strike the lion
and dust settles around the fallen flanks of so great

an animal king. He is my enemy, a mighty warrior
who challenges my turf. I move the sheep of my father
Jesse beyond the bluffs, past
the glittering hide, lions' dens and the smell of blood.
Even as I remember this, I manipulate the strings with

a song of triumph and skill. Out of the corner
of my eye, I see King Saul finger the edge of the
newly sharpened spear, slowly pick it up and study
its weight. He eyes an imaginary target, draws
back the spear, and I quickly disappear behind

another wall, still strumming as I hear the hum
of the spear where once I sat. The king's eyes
are possessed with hatred, though a false smile
diffuses his face. Even when his eyes are
closed by music, jealousy grips his troubled heart.

This, because, with the Lord's help, I extended his career.
I settle down again, to play the harp as the King says,
"Ah, that evil spirit torments me again. Play that quiet
Psalm, the one about still water and green pastures."
He settles into a cushion with a spear at his side, and

I recall the spear he lent me to use against the nine foot
Philistine who dared the Israeli army to come against
him, Philistine trumpet, bellowing across the Valley of Elah.
Father asked me to take some extra food to my brothers,
soldiers in the Israeli army, on my way back to work for

Saul. I was surprised to see a whole army quake in fear
against one who would defy the army of the Living God.
I polled the whispering soldiers to find that King Saul
would grant great wealth to the one who went up against
this armored hulk. Sizing him up, he was no bigger than

the bear who threatened my sheep a month ago.
Someone reported my questions to the King, who sent
for me. I offered to fight for the Lord against Goliath.
King Saul half-heartedly tried to dissuade me, meanwhile
fitting me with his own armor. He'd try anything at this

point. His reputation was at stake. Even though I had
been his minstrel-poet for many months, he did not
recognize me, and I could barely move in that hindering
armor, so I slipped out of it and stepped up to the
foul-mouthed heathen who was insulted by my boyish frame.

"Am I a dog," he exploded, "that you come to me with sticks
and stones?" My ears heard him roar like the grizzly
on his hind legs, rising above an army of quaking sheep.
I had rescued my sheep from the mouth of such a grizzly,
and this man's words against our God infuriated me more.

I watched his mouth move as I eyed my target above his nose.
Even to a grizzly I yell a battle cry, but to this unfearing man,
I yelled a calling card: "You come against me with sword
and spear and javelin, but I come against you in the name
of the Lord Almighty, the God of the armies of Israel,

whom you have defied." I wound the sling,
which wailed against the sky like a flute at dusk.
My sling sang the grizzled man to sleep.
He didn't just crumble; his nine feet fell like timber.

With the last note played, the once jeering Philistines tucked tail
and ran. The quaking Israeli army grew brave, pursuing
Philistine dust, while I carved a trophy for the King:
the head of Goliath using Goliath's own fifteen pound sword.
That was the end of Shepherding, for me. King Saul

was so relieved to have that man out of his way,
that he made me a high ranking officer in his army...as
long as I continued to visit between raids, kinnar in hand.
What brings me here to apply for this position is the King's
hatred for me. When Saul heard the townswomen singing

songs about me on the way to do their laundry, he listened
to the words. The song became a number one hit—every-
one knew it: "Saul has slain his thousands, and David
his tens of thousands." That's all it took for King Saul
to sense that I might be after his position (a position

promised to me as a young boy, but not yet mine).
Although he continued to be stricken by rage and needed
soothing music, he was more stricken by the sight
of me. As his employee, I still have to obey orders, whether
it is to go fight battles or sing songs. As I sing to him

now, the air is charged with his predictable fear. His
tall, fierce, rippled body lunges from the cushion as he
thrusts the spear in the direction of my music. Again,
I leap like a gazelle away from the offending instrument.
He recently demoted me to leader of a small band of

men in their campaigns against enemy troops. We've won
every skirmish, and my men are well-trained. I've come
to apply for the position of protecting your land,
my qualifications and my reputation are before you. Even
though I have killed your mighty warrior, Goliath, will

you accept me as your servant, King Achish, King
of the Philistines, as I continue my evasion of the raging
King of Israel? My men and I will set up housing outside
of this city to defend your borders, while we continue to
train for battle and practice the songs of sheep and of kings.

Homage

Blubber Tum (With apologies to Mr. Poe)

Once upon a midnight snacking as my lips were set to smacking
Over many a fatty morsel of salami and forgotten plum
While I snooped for snacks appealing, suddenly there came a feeling
As of someone softly stealing, stealing to my kitchendom.
"Tis some spoilsport," I muttered, "sneaking to my kitchendom."
Quoth the shadow, "Blubber Tum."

Ah, I thought. This must be Hubby, for he thinks that I'm too chubby.
And he thinks to catch me cheating, since no thinner I've become.
"Hon," I called, "I'm merely thawing out the icebox…I'm not gnawing…
For it kept me wide awake to think how sticky it's become."
Then I ceased, and heard the silence and the frigerator's hum.
Came the whisper, "Blubber Tum."

"That wee cake had been forgotten, and the cheese was turning rotten,"
I cried gaily. "I'd not think that you'd begrudge me but a crumb.
But come here…we both shall share it, for I simply could not bear it
If you thought I'd sneak a snack and try to hide it from my chum!
Do you think your wife so shifty she'd eat cake and then keep mum?"
Scoffed the shadow, "Blubber Tum."

"Lookee here, you Mr. Saintly," I burst out, though somewhat faintly.
"Did you think I had not noticed there's a donut gone, you bum?
And now you're here to quibble over one small measly nibble
That can scarce be seen when held betwixt my forefinger and thumb."
Then I licked a bit of frosting off the aforementioned thumb.
Quoth the shadow, "Blubber Tum!"

"Please! You're making me quite nervous. I have ice cream here I'll serve us
Drizzled o'er with nuts and chocolate. Look! There's more where that came from.
I no longer will deny it. I have gotten off my diet.
After this, on fatty foods there'll be a moratorium.
After this, I really promise," I said, feeling truly glum.
Spake my hubby, "Blubber Tum."

"Fiend!" I shrieked. "You hateful person! May your toenail fungus worsen.
May your dentist tell you jokes while drilling holes before you're numb!
May your razor leave you nubby. A huge pox on you, my hubby.
You forget who stirs the kettle in this little kitchendom!"
Now came hubby's early inkling of my deep opprobrium
For his heartless "Blubber Tum."

There is naught that could be blander than the sauce fixed for this gander
As he rues the night that prudence didn't warn him to keep mum
Though he finds the prospect galling, by the weekend he'll come crawling
He'll confess the rude name-calling was exceptionally dumb
Watch him practice saying humbly: "My! How slender you've become!"
Mr. Hum-bull, cut the "hum"!

So my husband, as is fitting, still is sitting; still is sitting
Gazing at the pallid salad with the turnip greens, quite bummed;
Thinking how it would be splendid if the whole affair were ended
Reading "Wedded Bliss For Dummies"—a "Don't Do" compendium
I will probably forgive him, but I'll make him suffer some
For that callous "Blubber Tum."

Eulogy

View the man in darkness dwelling, crimson
thoughts, abreast, instilling.
Pity he, the ebon, chilling, anguished, lost,
remorseful sigh.

See the sage in awful splendor, things of
grief, in sorrow, render.
Melancholy's bliss, remember, tortured
soul, with mem'ries wry.

Weep for Poe, the fallen angel! Hopes
triumphant, e'er to strangle.
Lost Lenore—your shade is tangled, ne'er to
him, will you be nigh!

Though your face of alabaster, stirred his
soul in hopeless rapture,
fickle gods, in judgment, captured,
thoughts of goodness, ne'er to die.

Cease Lenore, and end your haunting!
Leave him rest, and ever wanting.
E'er elusive, hunger vaunting, crooning
this, your sad repine.

Darknesses

Oh, how these Raven wings did fly
As they swooned in for a final dive,
Then did I hear a hushed voice cry;
Be not so brave,
When up so high…
For the ground now beckons,
And you've no fear to die.

I

Behold the Artist
And companion the Thinker
Force the medicine down their constricted throats
Lest the infection spread among the children of our Lord

Nary a word to question your substance
Yet you speak to us with your muddled thoughts

Return the Poets to their wards
They do not reflect our fine actions
They cannot recite our laws
They piss in the streets and dance until dawn
Their ways are strange
Their morals gone

You cover your walls with our passions
Your shelves fill with our lessons
You stare at us and wonder why
Your steps collide without grace
You cannot paint our likeness on your face

Do not attempt to smash the mirror
For you watch us there
and you watch us here
and we watch you exalt our places
You buy our wares to save our traces

Eccentric minds proliferate
Your wisest thoughts can always wait

Yet you cry out for morality
and feel pleasure in this
your complacency
We tempt you and disturb your truth
with no desire to be as you
This must reveal an err or clue
You stare aghast and look confused
We suffer not as fools
We do not need your rules

II

To the Artist
And companion the Thinker;
Step back through your cage!
We're frightened by each rabid phrase
Go back until you learn our ways
You are the whiskey we won't drink
You are the thoughts we dare not think

To the masses
We dare say
It's up to you to leave "your cage"
The one that locks your minds up tight
The one that lets you sleep at night
Our spirits wander and sometimes find
Others as fluid
Others as kind

You only recite what you have known
So leave behind your empty throne
Where no one sired a clever seed
Where cipher grew yet never conceived
Nor ever questioned why

Do stars speak at night to an empty sky?
Do you lust for life or wish to die?
Should you choose to follow our lead
To stalk the darkest pitch of eve
…you may repel all that you see

Your pain is buried
Our pain is carried…
From Artist to companion; The Thinker

III

My citizens of bronze
Cannot feel the wind
Imagine the rain
Wet on their skin

This is my Holy place
My Shadow Sanctuary
They won't look for me here
They won't find me at the Gates

And I feel no fear
I hear no Hate…I belong near
I wish I could die here
I wish for life here

A dead flower drapes from a vase
The arrangement is damp and vast
Neatly tie the stems
Hang to dry fast

We are the collective
Stand still and catch the castings
Kneel and wait in a solid state
Forever meant to last

I am a raindrop
So clear and round
No different than a teardrop
On the ground

IV

So here 'tis
The Autumn of a Prelude
Where every sadness in the world
Presses weight on these shoulders
Tears the size of boulders

Summer's curtain call
Fate bows to the Fall

Abuse my wants
Sever my needs
Lose my wishes
A subsequent please…

V

So this is Winter's feast
The fearless Solitaire
Chip off the Rosetta Stone

Take those I love
This Hell high above
Yet consider this
As proof I exist

No diamond without a flaw
In the rough I wait…so long
For sleep or daydreams
Or songs unsung…

I have many questions
For the strongest of glass
Who owns my forgiveness
Once lost, gone or past

Accept all my weakness
My famous collapse
The elusive Thrush
Sings a soloist gaffe

Last bird in the sky
Fly away fly…
Life must deny
Crystal glint return
Where fair love once burned

Twisting lone to glide
Sunset till Sunrise

In and Out of this World

The Ballad of the Eco-Rustlers

"The perimeter's been breached!" The alarm wailed. Chad Boswick jumped from his bunk. The CRT displayed a JPEG of the ranch. Three red lights blinked in the outer pastures. Two more dots blipped just outside the ranch's border. An icon indicated the presence of a hovercraft.

"God-damned eco-rustlers!"

Chad unplugged the Winchester from the recharging unit on the mantel. He threw an extra fuel cell in his holster. The computer confirmed that the life signs were rustlers. Chad checked his rifle. A green light flashed on the gun. The green light that authorized a kill.

The defense network calculated Chad's plan of attack. It fed the coordinates into his "black stallion," and forwarded his status to the Pinedale sheriff. The posse showed an ETA of thirteen minutes. Thirteen minutes! They wouldn't arrive on time!

The eco-rustlers, with their insipid vegan ways, had been working the western range for the last three years. Their insidious objective was nothing less than the complete destruction of the Wyoming cattle industry. Chad's quick draw was the last hope for the honest townsfolk of Pinedale.

He mounted his steed. He straightened his white hat. With an explosion of petrochemicals, Chad launched into the morning skies.

The lazy morning sun peeked from behind the jagged summits of the Windy Mountains, their peaks casting long dark shadows on the black clad rustlers. Chad circled above. The glint from the stallion's muffler caught a glance of their dark eyes.

Chad let go with three rapid shots. The first caught a rustler in the chest. Her right arm flew from her shattered body in a spiraling arc of pain-ridden death. The second shot ricocheted from a rustler's energy deflector as he high tailed it toward the barbed-wire fence. The final shot barreled into desert sage.

From a nearby hover craft the rustlers' gang fired a disrupter. The blast knocked Chad from his gallant steed. He tumbled to the ground below. Where's that damn posse? Chad's hand was broke and useless. With his tongue he flipped his rifle to maximum charge. The eco-gang's hover craft was already fleeing into morning haze. In a final burst of desperation, he emptied the weapon in the direction of the craft. The shots glistened in the sky, then crashed into the condominium complex in the foothills.

Where's that damn posse?

His wrist console showed an ETA of six minutes. The bad guys won again. Chad loaded the second cartridge in his gun.

He took a quick survey of the cattle. Seven of the beasts had been fitted with 'trodes. Oblivious to the searing pain of his sprained ankle, Chad ran toward the beasts. He tried to remove the 'trodes, but Chad's laptop confirmed that seven beasts were infected with the cogno-virus. The cattle were rapidly developing cognition. Chad had to work fast! The 'trodes were a diabolical tool of the eastern liberal elite. These strange devices, when planted in a cow's brain, would stimulate rapid neural activity, increasing the cattle's cognitive awareness. Once consciousness hit 0.75 AJOS (Average Joe On the Street), the 'trode would dial in and register the cattle with the Social Security Administration.

The 'trodes worked fast. Within a scant fifteen minutes of infection, one could bring a cow from prime grade beef to the worthless legal sentience. Once registered with the Federal Sentient Life Commission of the Social Security Office, the cattle were protected by the misguided, liberal National Sentient Statute of 2026, and could not be destroyed.

The only hope for the western town was to put the cattle down as quickly as possible. Chad aimed his rifle toward the closest beast. A green light flashed. He pulled the trigger. The gun hesitated. He yanked on the trigger again, it bucked once, then let forth with a thunderous blast.

A pale yellow light surrounded the eighteen hundred pounds of prime beef. The cow fell to the ground in spasmodic death. He aimed at the second cow, but the authorization light had turned red. A recorded voice from the gun spoke:

> "You are pointing this gun at an unarmed, registered
> sentient life form. According to our records, this life form is
> harmless and cannot be zapped into oblivion with this
> device. For more information please type [F1], or consult
> your user manual. Thank you for using the Winchester
> Zap-0-Matic Death Ray."

Chad yanked on the trigger to no avail. The cow stood back in terror. Chad clutched the weapon like a club, and rushed the cow.

Ouch!" said the cow, "Why is this ape-like creature hitting me with a stick? What have I done to be the focus of such anger?" The cow jumped back and plodded out of swinging range.

The five other sentient cows stared at Chad in utter amazement. They looked at the dead woman. They looked at her arm lying in a patch of purple larkspur.

Larkspur always causes stomachaches. A dead woman lying in Larkspur looked even less appetizing. The bull walked over and poked at the carcass of his comrade lying in the morning dew. The carcass had a 'trode protruding from its neck.

Was this 'trode the thing that suddenly gave them the ability to perceive and discuss their surroundings? What should they do about the human with a stick? What were those strange metal birds circling overhead? This was too much for the cows on their first day as registered rational beings. They stampeded away.

The posse was late. Three of the deputies dropped out of formation to check on the girl, the rest flew in the direction of the rustlers' vapor trail.

Chad looked in dismay at the retreating cattle. Twenty grand worth of prime beef wasted! Had he arrived seconds sooner, he could have at least slaughtered the cows before they developed enough neural pathways to become welfare collecting citizens of the United States.

It was another sad day for the honest hard working cow folk of the Western Range. How much longer could they survive the onslaught of the eco-rustlers? What good are cattle that discuss Plato? But, now was not the time for idle speculation. Chad spat into the dirt. He had some beef to slaughter.

The Purple Permanent

Wednesday was always a quiet day at Thrudmondo's Boutique de Coiffeur, but this particular Wednesday was especially so, mostly due to the unseasonable weather. It was not simply raining; it was quite literally pouring cats and dogs. Even for this particular town, which boasted an unusually high number of wizards residing within its precincts, a downpour of Yorkshire Terriers and Persian Blues was not considered an everyday occurrence. However, there was a perfectly logical reason for it all. More or less.

"You're going in and that's final," a voice could be heard saying in the street outside the shop. If a voice could have an edge to it, this one could have cut through six inches of tempered steel.

"But, Miranda, dearest…"

"Enough! In! And you, too. Stop trying to hide behind the parrot!"

"Boss, can't you reason with her? I don't need a—"

"Yes, you do. Now shut up, the pair of you, and get in there before I lose my temper!"

Through the door stepped a rather bedraggled wizard in mauve robes, accompanied by an equally disheveled youth who seemed to be constructed from all the knees and elbows left over from making several other people. A pretty blonde girl stepped from behind the reception desk to greet them.

"Can I help you, sirs?"

"Um…not really," muttered the wizard. "Must dash. Come along, Albert." He swiveled the youth around and turned back to the door, but the sight of a mauve-and-blue garbed sorceress standing outside the door, glaring in with an expression so frosty that it was beginning to ice up the glass, seemed to change his mind.

The wizard spun himself and his companion around once more. "Will you stop doing that?" protested the youth. "I'm starting to get dizzy!"

"Er…" began the wizard, a weak grin struggling to break through his beard, "I meant yes," he said. "The lad and I would like our hair cut. However, since you're probably very busy…"

"No, actually, we're not," said the girl. "We've had a lot of cancellations this morning, due to this odd weather."

"Yes," the wizard said slowly. "I wonder what could be responsible for that?" He glanced back outside. Perhaps…

"It's not worth it, boss. Miranda's still out there somewhere," his companion said.

The wizard sighed. "Oh, very well," he conceded. "Two for haircuts. Names of Mandaar the Mauve and Albert Albert. My apprentice," he added. "That's just in case you've formed any misguided impressions that this lanky streak of idleness is related to me or something equally embarrassing."

"If sirs will step this way…"

As they followed the girl to the waiting area, the youth, Albert, realized there was something distinctly odd about her. Perhaps it was the diamond-studded tiara holding her elegant golden locks in place. Or the multiple strings of pearls draped so carefully about her dainty neck. Or maybe, just maybe, it might have been the lapel pin on her overall, which read; "I'm Princess Clarissa. How may I help you?"

Some parents give their offspring the most ridiculous names, he mused. It was probably no worse than naming a son "Duke" or "Earl", but it must have been embarrassing at school. Being named Albert Albert had been bad enough!

"Who'd like to be first, please?" Princess Clarissa asked. Mandaar shrugged and followed her through a beaded curtain. Albert looked around for something to read, but two minutes of sifting through the magazines on offer convinced him that he would be better off counting the patterns on the wallpaper. Most were women's magazines, with nary a decent article about troll football or magic carpet maintenance to be found anywhere in their pages. Knitting patterns and cake recipes held little interest for him, and some of the other articles left him either red-faced with embarrassment or simply baffled. One magazine seemed obsessed with what Albert could only presume was interior plumbing of some sort. The article about something called a G-spot was puzzling enough, but he gave up altogether on one correspondent, who seemed to have found H, I, and J spots and finally something she described as a XYZYESYESYESSS spot.

An ear-splitting shriek suddenly shattered the relative silence. As the sound filtered through Albert's ears to his legs by way of his brain, millions of years of evolution took over and said legs propelled him off his seat and into a position more suited for shrinking the space between himself and the exit as rapidly as possible. However, as realization dawned that the scream had been in Mandaar's voice, his legs reluctantly relinquished control to his brain. He ought to investigate this. He would never hear the last of it if he didn't.

Hesitantly pushing his way through the curtain, he collided with the hairdresser coming the other way. "Please!" she begged. "Talk to him. It wasn't my fault!"

"What wasn't?" Albert asked from the floor.

"This wasn't!"

Albert looked up. The voice was Mandaar's, but surely the apparition speaking the words could not be he? Mandaar had shaggy white locks in need of a trim. He most certainly, in Albert's experience, had never sported a fuzzy purple perm before!

"Look what you've done to me, woman!" the wizard was shouting. "You've turned me into a freak! What the…"

What followed next would have been ordinary, if somewhat undesirable, words if uttered by anyone else but, Mandaar being a wizard, his expletives were accompanied by a stroboscopic lightshow which the average rock concert promoter would have killed for. This had the effect not only of turning the hairdresser's face bright pink, but also her hair, her overalls, her shoes and sundry other items not suitable for family viewing. Also, a thriving colony of cockroaches which had been resident in the building for some twenty years suddenly developed an urge to emigrate overseas and were never seen again.

"Just what in the name of the gods were you thinking of?" Mandaar concluded at length. The lightshow subsided and everything reverted to its normal hue—except for Mandaar's hair, which still looked like a purple cotton candy.

"I'm sorry," began the distraught girl, nervously playing with the lapel badge which proclaimed her to be 'Princess Clarissa'. "I…"

Whatever else she had intended to add was forgotten as a dapper man in an obvious wig came rushing through. The wig was obvious because, although it had carefully woven and lovingly colored to look like natural hair, the hair it had been matched to evidently belonged to someone other than the man actually wearing it. He blanched as he caught sight of Mandaar.

"Oh, no!" he cried. "It'sa happening again!"

"I'm sorry, Thrudmondo! I really am!" blurted the girl, and fled.

Again?" blustered Mandaar. "You mean this has happened before?" His eyes narrowed suggestively. "Well, you'd better have a good explanation for this!"

"Pleeese. The girl, she canna help it. Forgive her. She, 'ow you say? Under a curse."

Mandaar folded his arms. "All right, explain," he said slowly. "But first, drop that stupid accent. I know perfectly well that you were born three streets away from here and your real name is Smith!"

"I'ma sorry…I mean, sorry, guv," said Thrudmondo. He cleared his throat. "It's like this, see. Princess Clarissa, there, she 'ad this big-shot wizard fall in love with 'er, only she didn't love 'im back, know what I mean? So 'e put a curse on 'er. Put 'er under a compulsion to work as an 'umble 'airdresser until she agrees to marry 'im. Cept with 'er bein ensorcelled an all, whenever she works on anybody who knows a bit of magic, the curse sorta leaks a bit into the customer's 'air. Sorry."

"But why do you employ her if she keeps having this effect on people?" asked Albert, who had decided it was about time he got up from the floor.

"Well, it's the prestige thing, innit? 'Er dad's a king, an 'avin royalty on the staff's good for bizness. Course, their kingdom's so small that if the guard on the western border post sneezes, 'e gives 'is cold to everybody in the country to the east, but royal is royal, innit?"

"You mean she really is a princess?" Mandaar was skeptical.

"Yeah. Mind, that ain't the only reason. That wizard wot done for 'er's a nasty piece of work. If 'e got wind as I'd fired 'is lady love, I'd be in serious danger of gettin turned into a frog!"

"You still might be," said Mandaar, looming threateningly, "unless you do something about my hair."

"Can't," protested Thrudmondo. "It's a curse, see? Til it's lifted, all its effects are permanent. Short of cuttin the lot off, I can't do a thing about it."

"I see," said Mandaar. "In that case, I think I'd better have a word with this Princess Clarissa."

Five figures peeked cautiously out from between the gaps in a hedgerow. Well, strictly speaking, the previous sentence was not quite accurate. Five figures were behind the hedgerow, but only two were actually peeking out. Of the rest, one was sitting on Mandaar's shoulder and making a vain attempt at preening itself into something resembling a normal specimen of parrothood, another was nervously fiddling with a pair of scissors and desperately fighting back an almost overwhelming urge to work on Albert's split ends, while the last seemed to be paying no attention to anything, totally absorbed in a magazine article about the XYZYESYESYESSS spot.

"Is that where he lives, then?" asked Albert.

"Yes," replied Mandaar. "Typical of Norman the Colorless. Always did lack any sense of style. Who else would buy an eight hundred year old castle, pebble-dash the outer walls and rename it 'Dunroamin'?"

"Norman the Colorless? That's an odd name," commented Clarissa.

"Not really," said Mandaar. "It suits him perfectly. I remember him from our college days. He was less interesting than the average train spotter and almost as sophisticated. And indecisive…ye gods! I sometimes partnered him in Practical Alchemy classes. We were always last to finish, because he never could make up his mind whether to use, say, a crocodile spleen or bat's toenails. Hence the name. He couldn't even decide on a color. How he got to be a first-order wizard, I'll never know."

"So how did you get mixed up with him?" Albert said to Princess Clarissa, whom Mandaar had insisted on bringing along in spite of her protests.

"Oh, he did a job for Daddy," she explained. "Daddy hired him to rid us of a plague infesting the kingdom. The trouble was, even though it was only a little plague—of woodlice, actually—Norman insisted on the standard rate for the job."

"And what's that?" inquired Mandaar.

"Half the kingdom and the hand of the king's daughter," said Mandaar's wife Miranda, who was secretly paying attention after all. "Of course, in these enlightened times of political correctness, he might well have to settle for the hand of the king's son, but that's progress for you."

"Unfortunately, I'm an only child," said Clarissa. "Anyway, he didn't really want half the kingdom, even though Daddy offered him the half with the potting shed and the lawnmower in it, but he did insist on marrying me. Except I didn't want to get married. I was young, bright and healthy and I wanted to travel and see the world. I also wanted to learn a foreign language and work towards bringing the peoples of the world closer together in peace, harmony, and…"

"Yes, yes, we get the picture," said Mandaar. "Now, be quiet, will you? I'm looking for the best way in."

"I'd have thought the front door was fairly obvious," observed the princess. "Why are we hiding in the bushes, anyway?"

"We're not hiding," Miranda said. "We're lurking."

"It's the boss' policy," Albert explained. "He's always believed you should lurk before you leap."

Before Clarissa could make further comment, Mandaar stood up. "I've made a decision. Princess, put on that hooded cloak I gave you. We're going in."

"Have you figured out some devious way to gain entrance in secret, then?" asked Albert.

"Not quite," Mandaar admitted. "I thought we'd try the front door…"

"Ah, Mandaar! So good to see you, old fellow. How many years has it been, now? Love the hairdo. And this will be your lady wife, I presume?"

The interior of Castle Dunroamin bore no resemblance whatsoever to the picture Albert had had in mind before they entered. He had envisaged halls hung with faded tapestries and brooding portraits of past lords of the manor. He had imagined gleaming suits of armor, oak-paneled bookshelves, enormous chandeliers and, dominating everything, a roaring log fire overhung by a huge painting of a stag at bay. What he had not foreseen was the row of ducks in flight mounted on floral wallpaper in shades of gray, nor the off-white warped ceiling, the gray mock leather three-piece suite, the array of porcelain pigs on the mantelpiece over the gas heater, nor the plastic coffee table with the tacky lamp in which blobs of some unspeakable gelatinous goo undulated globulously up and down.

He had anticipated servants, of course, and, indeed, servants there were. However, smart but rather archaic and nonfunctional livery was not for the servants of Norman the Colorless. Instead, every one of them was clad in a baggy gray sweat suit with a multitude of pockets and a color-coded (if shades of gray can be considered colors) patch on the shoulder to denote his or her position.

Albert suppressed a sigh. All in all, he felt this was one of the most characterless, lackluster, soulless places he had ever had the misfortune to set foot in.

"Sit down, please. Make yourselves comfortable," Norman was saying. Even his voice was colorless and drab, the sort of voice which gave people an almost overwhelming urge to get up, leave him to it and go and make a cup of tea. "Is that your familiar, Mandaar?" he continued. "My, what a coincidence. I have a parrot, too. Parrot!"

In response to Norman's shout, a large parrot—gray, naturally—flew in through an open doorway and perched on the back of the sofa. Mandaar's familiar, Gervase, who had looked up to this point as though he was about to fall asleep, suddenly perked up.

"Who's a pretty boy, then? Awk!" squawked the gray parrot. This should prove interesting, thought Albert. As he watched, Gervase's beak seemed almost to curl upwards in a sneer.

"Kukkkk…" said Gervase, somehow making it sound ominously like a snarl. He hopped from Mandaar's shoulder onto the sofa back and glared at the gray parrot, which suddenly looked extremely worried.

Mandaar seemed oblivious to all this. As one of the servants brought in a crudely-enameled tin tea tray with a badly-painted picture of Little-Belching-On-Sea harbor on it, Mandaar waved it away.

"I'll come straight to the point, Norman," he said. "I want you to do something about this." He removed his wizard's hat and pointed to the purple frizz billowing out of his head like a dandelion clock on hallucinogenic drugs.

Norman the Colorless looked puzzled. "Sorry?" he said.

"This mess on my head," said Mandaar. "Thrudmondo's? Princess Clarissa? Ring any bells?"

"Ah!" exclaimed Norman, comprehension dawning in his almost translucent eyes. "Yes, I understand. Mmm…how unfortunate. My dear chap, I do apologize."

"Apologize? Look, Norman, that won't do. I insist that you change my hair back to normal immediately and then lift this stupid curse. I'm not the first victim, am I? Thrudmondo tells me there have been at least six others. It's got to stop! This sort of thing gives wizards a bad name."

A sly expression weaseled its way across Norman's sallow face. "I'm afraid it's not quite as simple as that, old chap. Debt of honor, you see. Owed half her father's kingdom and her hand. Standard rates and all."

"Well, at least put my husband's hair back to normal," said Miranda, speaking for the first time. "You can sort out this 'debt-of-honor' business afterwards, but I'm getting rather tired of being married to someone who looks like a frizzy blackcurrant lollipop!"

Mandaar looked slightly wounded but held his tongue as Norman walked around him, looking him over, shaking his head and sucking in his breath.

"Well," Norman said at length. He made a clicking noise with his tongue. "I don't know. If it was bangs, or a ponytail, or even a crew cut, I could perhaps change you back, but with this lot I'm afraid the only option is to shave it all off and let it grow again."

"Not on your life!" said Miranda. "The purple mop look is bad enough, but I'm not going to have him looking like a wing nut in a robe!"

"But it's because it's curls, you see. I could change any normal masculine style, but it's different for curls…"

"Masculine?!" choked Mandaar.

At this point, Albert realized it had gone very quiet on the other side of the room, and he ventured a look around to see what Gervase was up to. Somehow, the gray parrot had become lashed around the stem of a table lamp standing on a badly-assembled do-it-yourself-kit sideboard by the window. Gervase was nowhere to be seen.

"Right, then," Mandaar declared, rolling up his sleeves in the time-honored manner of magicians everywhere before performing a feat of magic. "Time to stop talking and start acting. Lift the curse, Norman. It's a stupid curse, anyway."

"No, it isn't!" Norman said defensively. "It was a move guaranteed to bring Clarissa to the brink of despair, so that she will realize she can find happiness again by marrying me. I've heard the warning the Hairdresser's Guild gives to all newcomers to the profession; 'Abandon hope all ye who enter Hair!' It's a soulless, thankless way of life. Everybody knows that."

"Who cares? Just lift the curse."

"No. Not until Princess Clarissa agrees to marry me!"

"That does it!" said Miranda. "Clarissa isn't some object you can barter for, she's a human being with feelings and rights. There isn't any way she's going to marry you if I have any say in the matter."

Clarissa, hidden under the cloak Mandaar had lent her, had stood almost motionless since entering Castle Dunroamin, although little tell-tale movements of her head suggested she was taking detailed stock of her surroundings. Now she moved forward and tugged on Miranda's robe. "Excuse me…"

"Not now, dear," whispered Miranda. "Well, Norman? Are you going to lift the curse or not?"

"No!" screamed Norman. He gestured, and a dull but deadly-looking lightning bolt flashed from his fingertips towards Mandaar.

"Princess Clarissa must marry me!" howled Norman the Colorless.

"The hell she must!" responded Mandaar. With one hand, he deflected the lightning to strike a painting on the opposite wall, which depicted several dogs playing pool. From his other hand, a purple fireball sprang to life and shot towards Norman.

"Stop them!" shrieked Clarissa.

"Sorry, dear," said Miranda, calmly. "It's against all the rules of wizardly conduct to interfere in a magical duel. Although," she added with a wry twist to her lips, "if Mandaar loses, that's a different matter." She ushered Clarissa back behind the sofa, almost tripping over Albert, who had transferred himself there at the first sign of trouble so fast that he did not seem to have ever occupied the space in between.

"Oh, get up, Albert," said Miranda. "Men! Either fighting or hiding. And you can stop that, too!" This last was directed towards Gervase, who had found some straw from somewhere and had stacked it around the gray parrot's feet. Until Miranda had spoken, he had been advancing purposefully upon the other bird with a tiny flaming torch clasped in his beak. Now, he dropped the torch and tried to look nonchalant.

Tutting, Miranda gestured and the string tethering the gray vanished. The parrot fled for its life with a speed which made Albert's progress to the back of the sofa seem like a funeral procession by comparison.

Meanwhile, the magical duel seemed to be stalemated. Phantasmal shapes flickered and howled between the two wizards and, although the duelists themselves seemed to be taking no harm, the same could not be said for the furnishings. The ducks in flight had vanished, and Albert could have sworn something had fled past his ear through the open window. Several somethings—which quacked! In addition, the dogs were no longer to be seen on what was left of the large painting, although several floppy ears could be observed twitching behind the pool table. Elsewhere, vases of flowers were turning to doves and canes, chairs were getting up and running out of the room as fast as their four legs could carry them, and even the globular table lamp suddenly took off with an explosive roar and rocketed through the ceiling, bringing down a copious shower of plaster.

"No!" Princess Clarissa exclaimed. "No, this is too much! They'll ruin everything!" She suddenly shot away from Miranda and interposed herself between the two male wizards. Mandaar reacted instantly, aborting the spell he had been casting. The enormous winged snake which had been in the process of materializing in front of him looked momentarily startled before disappearing up its own left nostril.

Norman also froze in mid-gesture. "Do you mind?" he grumped. "Can't you see we're in the middle of a duel?"

Clarissa threw back her hood. "But you must stop!" she declared. "You're destroying this beautiful room!"

"Beautiful?" chorused Mandaar, Miranda and Albert together. Even Gervase looked nonplussed and gave a surprised, "Kukkk...?"

"Your highness!" exclaimed Norman as he recognized her. "Mandaar, how could you place the woman I love in such peril?"

"You started it," said Miranda, placing a protective arm around Clarissa. "All right, Norman, enough is enough. Clarissa isn't going to marry you, so lift this stupid curse and be done with it, eh? Otherwise, rules or no rules, I'll add my powers to Mandaar's against you. You can't defeat both of us together!"

"But..." began Clarissa.

"Hush. Well, Norman?"

Norman bowed his head, crestfallen. "Very well. I..."

"No!" cried Clarissa. She broke away from Miranda and rushed to Norman's side. "Leave him alone, you—you bullies, you!"

"What do you think you're doing?" asked Mandaar.

"Very simple," said Clarissa. "Norman and I are going to get married, aren't we, darling?"

Norman offered no reply. He looked as bewildered as everybody else.

"You can't!" Miranda said. "Princess, you can't marry someone just because they've put a curse on you."

"Why not?" Clarissa said. "I love Norman. I didn't know it before, but since we've been here I've discovered how much I've come to enjoy being a hairdresser.

Norman didn't curse me, he did me a favor. Also," she added, "I hadn't realized what impeccable taste he had."

"Are you sure he didn't curse your eyesight as well?" muttered Albert.

Clarissa ignored the interruption. "I just couldn't go back to being a boring princess after the joys of styling hair," she said. "Especially now I have the chance to live in such beautiful surroundings with a man who loves me."

"Yes, but what about my hair?" Mandaar reminded her.

"Oh, I can take care of that easily enough," said Norman, who seemed to have finally recovered his wits. "I'll just lift the curse and recast it. If that's what my darling really wants?"

"I do, I do! I want to spend the rest of my life married to you and mending split ends. Although," she added thoughtfully, "we'd better have a 'no wizards' policy in our new salon."

Mandaar shook his head. "Mad. Completely mad, the pair of them."

"Oh, I don't know," said Miranda, shrugging. "Neither Norman's plan nor yours went quite as you intended, but in the end everyone has what they really wanted. It only goes to prove the old saying," she added, "that the curse of true love never does run smooth!"

The Purple Punnet

Wizards have rather eccentric tastes. This is exemplified by the fact that no other group of individuals would consider a stuffed alligator to be an essential ceiling orna- ment. "It's not as if alligators can even fly," Albert, apprentice to Mandaar the Mauve, was often heard to complain. "If it was model flying carpets, I could under- stand it. Or even stuffed birds…" This last remark was usually accompanied by an evil glance in the direction of Gervase, Mandaar's familiar, a notoriously unkempt parrot who seemed to consider the stuffed alligator to be a sort of aerial toilet.

Mandaar's tastes in other areas also left much to be desired. The entire house was decorated in shades of mauve, purple and violet, just in case someone hap- pened to forget what Mandaar's name was. Where most people would have dis- played attractive ornaments, Mandaar kept all manner of 'conversation pieces' that he and his wife Miranda had picked up on their travels on the off chance that some day a use might be found for them. What use anyone could ever find for a collection of invisible left-handed toothpicks or a 500-year-old lizard's eyeball was beyond Albert, however. He dreaded dusting. It gave him nightmares.

There was just one area in which Albert's tastes did coincide with those of his employer. All practitioners of magic love strawberries, and Albert, despite having all the magical aptitude of a tin of sardines, was no exception. But there had to be a snag, of course.

"I don't see why I have to go out and pick the things by hand," he protested as Mandaar levitated a huge purple punnet into his hands and a floppy sun hat onto his head. "I mean, you're a top-notch wizard, boss. Why can't you just," He waved his hands in a vague approximation of a magical gesture. "Well, magic some strawberries or something? It can't be that hard."

Mandaar rolled his eyes skyward. "It isn't. But real, fresh strawberries taste better than magically created ones. Anyway, I don't hear you complaining when you eat them."

"Besides," added Miranda, glancing up from the magazine she was poring over at the breakfast table, "the words of the spell for creating strawberries are so dreadfully silly. All that 'ri-ful, ri-ful, fol-der-iddle-idle' nonsense."

"But…"

"No more arguments," snapped Mandaar. "Not unless you want to spend the morning on a lily pad catching flies. Off you go!"

"Can I take the carpet?" Albert asked.

"No. It's only a couple of miles. Walk. The exercise will do you good."

"And take the parrot with you," added Miranda, without looking up from her magazine. "He could use some exercise as well."

Gervase glared evilly down at Albert from his much-splattered perch atop the stuffed alligator. "Come to daddy, Gervaseykins," said Mandaar. "Let me take you down, cause Albert's going to the strawberry fields."

"Oh, thanks," muttered Albert, returning the parrot's death-stare. "Thanks a bunch."

Needless to say, the only exercise, which Gervase indulged in on the way, involved the muscles of his toes as he dug his claws into Albert's shoulder. The air around Albert, meanwhile, grew ever more blue as he walked the two miles or so to the strawberry farm. By the time he reached his destination, he was biting his tongue to stop himself from swearing, as the air was now a deep indigo and he could barely see where he was going.

There were already people at work in the fields, he noted, mostly other apprentices, the other local wizards having had much the same idea as Mandaar this morning. He stood at the gate for a minute or two, allowing the air to regain its normal translucency and taking in the delicious aroma of fresh strawberries wafting on the breeze. The place had a magical quality of its own, almost as if nothing was real. There seemed to be strawberry fields forever in every direction.

"Well, let's make a start," he decided, picking a row. "And I'm warning you, bird," he growled at Gervase as the parrot hopped from his shoulder onto the handle of the punnet. "No stuffing the things into your beak as fast as I pick them."

"Kukkk," replied Gervase innocently, greedily eyeing up the plump red fruits as Albert started picking.

Two hours later, at least half of which had been spent in beating off Gervase with a stick to stop him scoffing the lot, Albert hauled a punnet filled to over-flowing with strawberries over to the hut near the gate, which served as a vending booth.

"My, that's a lot of strawberries," the girl in the hut said. She made a pass over the punnet and muttered a brief weighing spell. "That'll be two and a half silver pieces, please."

"Don't I know you from somewhere?" Albert asked as he handed over the money Mandaar had given him. "I do, don't I? You were at the Apprentice's Ball last year. You're apprenticed to…let me see…"

"To Roseanne the Red-And-Green-With-Odd-Little-Yellow-Bits," the girl replied with a slight blush. "My name's Katrina. You're Albert, aren't you?"

"Wow!" said Albert, his own blush managing to outshine the strawberries. "You remember me. Uh…" he suddenly found himself stuck for words. "Um…so what are you doing working here?"

Katrina smiled. "Oh, this is just a part-time job to earn myself enough to go on to college after I finish my apprenticeship."

Albert's mind suddenly boggled. Finish her apprenticeship? He had never given much thought to finishing his own. To be honest, he was so useless at magic that he envisaged himself still being an apprentice at an age when most people qualified for a free enchanted coach pass. He suddenly lost the urge to continue this conversation.

"Um…got to go. See you," he mumbled, picking up his punnet and hurrying away. "That does it!" he said. "I'm going to have to see the boss about teaching me some proper spells, or at this rate the most useful one for me is going to be conjuring up a magic zimmer frame!"

Behind him, Katrina's smile twisted into a smug grin.

"Where is he? I'll kill him!"

"Calm down, Mandaar. I'm sure there's a perfectly reasonable explanation."

Mandaar glared at his wife, a gesture that went completely unnoticed as Miranda was hidden behind the latest issue of *Witches' Realm* and absorbed in an article on 'A Hundred and One Interesting Things To Do With Newts' Nostrils'.

"Look, will you at least pay attention while I'm trying to have a screaming row with you? How could there be a reasonable explanation for this?"

Sighing, Miranda put her magazine down and regarded the object in her husband's shaking hands. "Well, it isn't necessarily Albert's fault," she offered, casting a glance at the ceiling to the stuffed alligator.

"Don't try to blame Gervase. He's totally innocent. Just look at him." Miranda looked. Sure enough, Gervase was perched innocently atop the stuffed alligator, trying his best to look angelic. He could hardly look anything else, dressed up in a parrot-sized choirboy's robe with his wings pressed together in front of him.

"All right, Gervase. Point taken," she said. "Don't get carried away." She turned back to Mandaar. "Why don't you just ask Albert? Get his side of the story before you condemn him."

"I would if I could find him. But…just a moment!" A tiny flake of plaster drifted floorward. "I see…"

Muttering a quick spell, Mandaar rose into the air until he was level with the stuffed alligator. "Um, hello, boss," said a familiar voice. "Just thought I'd do a bit of dusting up here."

Now, given that Mandaar's stuffed alligator was about four feet long and eighteen inches wide, and that Albert was a gangling five feet eleven in his socks, one might consider that it would take an amazing feat of contortionism to conceal the latter atop the former, especially when competing for space with a belligerent purple parrot. However, this was lost on Mandaar as he grabbed his apprentice by the scruff of the neck and hauled him to the ground.

"All right, Wart," the wizard growled, using the time-honored nominative that allows apprentices to *know* that they're in trouble. "You've got five seconds to explain the meaning of this!" He waved a familiar object under Albert's trembling nose.

"It's a punnet," said Albert.

"Correction. It's an empty punnet."

"Not quite, boss. There are still a few strawberries left. Look."

"Right. Four, to be precise. So where are all the rest?"

"Um...you ate them?"

"We certainly didn't eat them," said Miranda. "Mandaar found the punnet like that just a few minutes ago."

"So where are they?" repeated Mandaar. "Have you eaten them? Or is this all you picked, you idle little..."

"No!" howled Albert. "It wasn't me, honest! The basket was full when I last saw it. Gervase must've eaten them."

"We've already been through that!" snapped the wizard, with a brief glance at Gervase, who had now added a bishop's miter to his outfit and was pounding out "All Things Bright And Beautiful" on a miniature harpsichord. "It must have been you. Why don't you admit it?"

Mandaar's tirade of abuse was cut off by a ringing sound from the crystal ball on the table.

"I'll get it," said Miranda. "Just keep the noise down, please."

Mandaar grunted and tightened his grip on Albert's throat as his wife spoke into the crystal. After a few exchanges, she covered it over with a cloth and turned to her husband. "That was Gronnle the Greenish-Beige," she said. "Guess what?"

"If he's come up with yet another of his famous hangover cures, I am not volunteering to try them out again," said Mandaar. "I still haven't recovered from the last one—eating a live cockroach between drinks."

"It worked, though, didn't it?"

"Only because it put you off drinking! Well? What did he want?"

"He's had a robbery. He sent his apprentice to pick some strawberries this morning and they've disappeared."

"What?"

"Don't you think you'd better put Albert down, dear? He's going a very strange color."

Mandaar released his grip and Albert staggered back, desperately trying to remember how to breathe. "Ruddy heck, boss!" he wheezed. "I did try to tell you it wasn't me."

"Shut up," said Mandaar, sitting down and stroking his beard. "And don't be such a baby. It's only air." He turned the punnet around, examining it closely. "There's a mystery here. Miranda, have you got a ferret's foot?"

"No, that's just the way I walk," joked Miranda. Her reward was a frosty glare from the two men. "Oh, all right, here you are," she said, dipping into her bag of spell ingredients.

Mandaar waved the ferret's foot over the punnet and muttered some magic words.

"I thought so. This has been hexed."

"Hexed, boss?" asked Albert, whose lungs had by now remembered what they were for.

"Hexed. Some conniving little so-and-so has cast a delayed teleportation hex on my punnet and transported the strawberries somewhere else."

"And whoever is responsible seems to have pulled the same trick on Gronnle the Greenish-Beige," said Miranda.

"Correct," agreed Mandaar. "Well, I'm going to get to the bottom of this. Pass me the crystal ball, Miranda," he said. "I've a few calls to make."

"Delicious strawberries."

"Mmm. Scrumptious. A bit pricey, though."

"Well, you pay for quality. Besides, no one else around these parts seems to have any decent ones. It's all those wizards, you see. They can't resist them. They usually buy them all up before we get here."

"Well, gentlemen?" Katrina looked from one of the two men to the other. "Are they of the quality you're looking for? Will Mr. Monty purchase them?"

"Oh, very much so," said one of the men, stuffing another one into his mouth as he spoke. "Delbert Monty's Juices and Preserves & Trade, Inc. insists upon only the most succulent fruit, and these do meet our standards. I am most impressed. What do you say, Sidney?"

"Mmmf grmffl," replied the other man, nodding enthusiastically with a mouthful of strawberries.

Katrina beamed. "Then the men from Del Monty, they say…"

"Gangway, gangway. 'Scuse me. Make way."

The two purchasers from Delbert Monty & Trade, Inc. were rudely shoved aside as two men in purple overalls pushed through to the counter.

"Do you mind?" Katrina asked. "Please wait your turn. I'm serving these two gentlemen."

"Oh, can't do that, love, can we? Eh, Nobby?" said the older of the two newcomers, a slightly corpulent man with a white beard.

His youthful, awkward-looking companion nodded. "Government health inspectors, see."

"What did he say, Sidney?" said one of the two men from Delbert Monty & Trade, Inc.

"Something about elf inspectors," replied Sidney. "Funny. I can't see any elves to inspect, can you?"

"We're health inspectors. *Health!*," repeated the skinny man for their benefit. "I'm sorry, but we'll have to close this booth down. There's been an outbreak of…of, er…"

"…of crocodilius saginarus," the man with the beard finished for him. "Highly contagious, you know."

"Oh, dear," said Sidney.

"Oh, dearie dear," agreed his companion. They both started to sidle backwards a few steps, then turned and kept on going, accelerating with every step.

"Now see what you've done," scowled Katrina. "I was just about to close a very lucrative deal with those men. They were from Delbert Monty & Trade, Inc, you know." She squinted at the two 'health inspectors'. "Just a minute. It's Mandaar the Mauve, isn't it?"

"Damn," fumed the bearded wizard. "How did you know?"

"Well, the wizard's hat and the parrot on your shoulder are a bit of a giveaway. Just what do you think you're doing, scaring off my customers like that? And don't give me any more of that 'health scare' rubbish. I know perfectly well that 'crocodilius saginarus' means 'stuffed alligator'."

"All right, since our game's up," said Mandaar, "you might as well know it's up for you as well. We're onto your little scheme. We know those strawberries you've got back here are all stolen."

"I don't know what you mean," said Katrina innocently. "They were picked fresh this morning from these very fields."

"Of course they were. However, they were picked by a couple of dozen wizards' apprentices, and then appropriated by you using Prufgrondler's Wondrous Linking Hex. It's an ingenious spell. You cast it on a container to link it to a second one. Nothing happens while the first container is being carried, but five minutes after it's put down, most of its contents are whisked away and reappear in the second one! Let's see…" He leaned over the counter. "I'll bet the spell is on your weighing table. And isn't that a nice, large basket underneath it? Just the thing to use as a receiver, I'd say."

Katrina sneered. "You'll never prove it. And before you get any ideas about coming in here and examining my basket, you'd better have a police search warrant. Otherwise you can get lost."

"And of course, by the time we do get the police here with a warrant, the hex will have been conveniently removed."

"What hex?" she asked with poisoned sweetness.

Mandaar ignored her. "What's the time, Albert?"

Albert glanced at his wrist sundial. "We're cutting it a bit fine, boss. Just over a minute to go." He looked worried.

"Long enough," said Mandaar. "All right, Katrina, you may have seen through our disguises, but I do have a backup plan. You see, before I came here I called all of the other wizards you swindled this morning. Over two dozen of them, all with hexed punnets linked to that basket under your table."

"Allegedly," said Katrina. "And so what?"

"Boss…" Albert began nervously.

"Point taken," said Mandaar. "Okay, run for it!"

Albert did not have to be warned twice. Before Mandaar had completed the exclamation mark, his apprentice was halfway up the field and about to overtake the two men from Delbert Monty & Trade, Inc. Mandaar tutted, waved his arms and he andGervase vanished, to reappear a few feet in front of Albert.

"Show-off!" was all Albert had time to mutter before he collided with his employer and they went down in a heap.

Katrina watched all this with a bemused expression. What did those two clowns think they were doing?

There was a *plink!* sound from behind her. She turned. Odd, but that sounded like something dropping into the basket under the table. But it couldn't be. Could it? There was another *plink!* sound, and another…

Then the hut exploded.

Albert could not resist looking up as assorted bric-a-brac showered outwards from the remains of the booth in all directions. It included old clothes, broken pottery, empty cans and bottles and boxes, half the contents of a compost heap, magazines and newspapers, an elephant's-foot umbrella stand and a confused and terrified black cat, which swiveled in mid-air, landed on its feet and bolted away at approximately twice the speed of sound. There was also a familiar-looking stuffed alligator. Uh-oh, thought Albert. The boss isn't going to like that. Still, Miranda never could stand the thing.

Thrown clear, Katrina stared back with an aghast expression at what little remained of her hut. Then she got to her feet, shook her head and gave a shrill whistle. A broomstick shot from the wreckage and came to a hovering halt inches from where she was standing. Hiking up her skirt, she glanced nervously towards Mandaar and Albert and then started to mount the broom—just as the stuffed alligator, having given the lie to Albert's claim that it was incapable of flight, came plummeting from the sky to land on her head. All 139 pounds of it.

Mandaar strolled casually towards where she lay, followed by Albert and the two shell-shocked men from Del Monty & Trade, Inc. Katrina stirred as they reached her.

"Uhhh," she groaned. "What happened?"

"You got too greedy, that's what happened," Mandaar said, helping her to her feet. "About five minutes ago, all those other wizards I mentioned started stuffing things into the punnets you had hexed. Of course, since you only had one receiving container, everything arrived in it at the same time. And you can see the result." He indicated the debris all around with one sweeping hand motion.

Katrina moaned again. "I suppose that's that, then."

"It certainly is," Mandaar said. "You made a mistake in linking all those punnets to a single receptacle. You should have used more than one container at this end. In other words," he grinned, "you shouldn't have put all your hex in one basket!"

Sketching Earthly Landscapes

One Orange Morning

I woke up one orange morning to discover a butterfly at my window.
As it bobbed and wove, it placed me in a daze.
Its hues; violent violet, majestic saffron, and a splash of teal were aglow.
My consciousness, like a pendulum, oscillated between clarity and haze.

This mesmerizing creature flew up towards the fiery disk in the sky.
As it dissolved into the warm golden rays, a gentle breeze beckoned.
With baled fists, I rubbed my eyes then looked at the spectacle gone awry.
A dove-shaped flame danced on the horizon for a split second.

In a blink of an eye the vision was no more.
I yawned, running my fingers through my woolly mane.
Looking Einsteinish, I paced the creaking, hardwood floor.
With fortified resolve I began my day with an ominous smile as I
glanced back at the window pane.

A Countryman's Song of the Seasons

Sing me a song of springtime
When the blossom hangs heavy on tree
And the celandine, aconite and wood violet,
Bloom sweetly for all to see.

Sing me a song of summer
When the sun rides high in the sky
And the fields are wet with dew and mist
And the lark sings gaily on high

Sing me a song of harvest
When the wains are piled high with corn
Drawn home by gentle shire horses
Who've worked to twilight, from dawn.

Sing me a song of autumn
When leaves fall russet and gold
And cobwebs sparkle with diamonds
On hedgerows frosted with cold.

Sing me a song of winter
When snow lies deep all around
And icicles hang from roof-top tree
And nothing stirs in the ground.

Leaves

I've seen the leaves fall now for many days—multi-colored hues reflecting all the prisms of sunlight, as they fall silently, swirling to the earth from their lofty home.

I wonder at times why so few notice the passage of these leaves? Some fall withered-their once vibrant texture has been ravaged by the wind and merciless elements.

Others slip prematurely from the mother-branch just as the act of photosynthesis begins to awaken them. They are little more than half-grown protuberances, immaturity all too obvious on their tender buds.

A few more leaves drop unexpectedly from great heights—they float, spiraling down, ever downward, until they kiss the harsh earth and join their muted brethren.

All the leaves are still. The green lay with the brown, the brown the red. Can anyone tell me just how many leaves have fallen? I must know, for it is my task to rake them up.

How many more leaves must fall?

Snow from the Heavens

Snow arrived like the Bible said it would,
Blowing strong and cold all night,
Merging earth and sky in a sea of paleness…
A moment rarely felt in this world of artificial light.

Snow rolled in waves west to east,
Encoding everything in its path,
A spirit searching for a final resting place
In star-grained space far beyond us.

This was a moonless, high, white, and swirling time
To fight through deep, rich, swirling dunes
Under stars I know are there, but cannot see
To a road unplowed for years to come.

Tracks tough to make and sunk so deep
Were lost without a trace in the moment required
To ascend the path with bowed head
And with bowed head trek back.

Walk upon the frozen ground and listen to it speak.

Birdfeeder Morning

A fresh flaky
four inch snow cover.
Bright early sun, crisp air.
Ice in bathroom water buckets.
Feed cats, rabbits.
Brush off hanging feeders.
Wood stove hot.
Coffee steaming,
sourdough toast.
Poetry.

The feast sits heavy
in one's stomach
while outside
chickadees eat
sunflower seeds.

Harken to the Silence

Listen to the silence.
Listen to its beat.
It has a profoundness
Neither form nor texture can define.

It's finely sculptured vision
That has no sound.
It's a dewdrop cradled in the grasses
Flashing colored brilliance
That has no sound.
It's sitting by a stream
Where everything is still.
It's walking in a deep forest.
Darkness is what you'll hear.

Listen to the silence
And its peaceful quiet.

Goodnight

The sun sails
Across billowy clouds
As it journeys west
The star of nature's show
Takes its curtain of blue
Wherever it goes
And in the night
Its light the moon reflects
Cat sits in the gentle breeze
Sees what only cat-eyes see
I look up into the night
At billions of flickering
Far away lights
Cat looks at me
Then slips out of sight
Before I go indoors
I say "goodnight."

Metamorphosis

Bird

What jeweler transformed this fanciful bird,
That once flew over colorful, blooming gardens,
Into the trapped shape of my pin?
Did he use cobwebs, ashes and fire to cast his spell?

Every high arch, bow, and curvature
Of the lyre bird's tail, now dazzles the eye.

Myriads of diamonds: Round brilliants, teardrops,
Even marquis, crowd each other for space
Along every curving, swerving feather.

Sweeping lines of light,
Fiery light, emanates from the glittering bird.

He's ornate magnificent, lavish, and jeweled.
Weighed down, instantly, by his new gold body,
Held in bondage, unable to fly,
The exotic bird awaits for the spell to be broken.

Chrysalis

I walked along that tarmac of leafy greenness,
knowing that all along while others were there
Hovering around me, dancing and loving life,
I was alone in my journey, oblivious to fan fare.

The warm arms of morning sun chased away the dew
Which threatened the very womb for which I spun and toiled.
For each fragile thread covered a piece of my lonely sordid past;
Suspended in time and place, purgatory unspoiled.

God created another road for my restless spirit,
When songs of life seeped through my fabric of death.
Faith tugged the sleeve of courage to break me from contentment;
The sabbatical of self pity ended in bated breath.

I broke loose from those sticky old walls of what was,
Imagine my surprise when I reached out to the sky,
And basked in the glow of a gallant new heart.
I had wings! I found freedom! I was able to fly!

I met others who journeyed as I once did from below.
Now full of color, and dancing, and living our best.
Gathering for the great exodus flight, southward, smarter,
Winking at chrysalises, knowing each is unaware they too are blessed.

A Whispering Thought

A still voice in my head
Soft as a whisper blowing through my mind
My thoughts float back to a simpler place and time

Rising early, we worked the farm
The feel of sticky tobacco leaves
Feeling the sun upon your back
Walking barefoot through the dirt of the earth

The sweet tender taste of biting into a red, ripe tomato
Fresh from the vine
A neighbor knocks on the door
Sits at your table for a cup of coffee
And for a bit of conversation

Sitting on the porch after dark
A clear sky, star gazing
Feeling a cool breeze gently touch your face

My mind returns to the present
And I tuck my memory away
For yet another time, another day
When I'll again hear the whisper
Blowing gently through my mind

Fear

It's always been there.
Hiding in the dark corners of my mind.
Silently it crept on me,
like a thick, black, too warm blanket.

I always knew it was there.
I held it at bay,
convincing it I was the stronger one between the two of us.

How was I to know it would slither in when my guard was down,
in my sleep.
Completely uninvited,
and equally unexpected.

For years it couldn't reach me,
and then it found me.

What was I thinking?

I obviously let my guard down,
looked away for a brief moment,
was concentrating too much on the wrong things.

Whatever I did or didn't do;
it found me and now I have to reclaim my independence.
Come face to face with these shadows.

Shadows on the Ceiling

The door to my room is closed, soft music playing
The curtains pulled, the shades drawn
Closed away from the world, alone with my thoughts
Making shadows on the ceiling, like the shadows of my life
The years pass so quickly; our time slips away
Just like the blades of the fan
Going by in rapid succession, one turn after another
Another year passes and I wonder where it went
There it goes and along with it
All those things I planned to do
Another year, another wish and dream gone
I think of those dreams and how someday
They might actually come true, if I work and believe
The thoughts flit back and forth in my mind
Like the fan turning on the ceiling
But, it's late and past time for bed
I turn off the music, lie down and turn off the light
Say a prayer before sleep
For a good day tomorrow

Waiting

Alone on the porch, an icy drink at hand.
A few moments to be in no one's presence

A voluptuous breeze pushes through tired tree limbs,
catching my face, my hair, breathing wakefulness into my mind.

Placid night, warmth light, easy breathing, to take my cares,
pushing them to better places away.

I relish this, my quiet security, paying a peaceful homage,
homage to the fact that I have left the rust of anger behind.

No holding grudges, no vengeance, this is not mine.

Sweet moments, where you least expect them, repay me in full.
I am rich, many are, more are not

You, my friend, you are rich if you even have the time;
Time to sit and read, think or work at nothing.

Riches are not always added in the same way,
and contentment is sought by many more than have found it.

Search until you have found the greater love,
hold on to the brink of almost nothingness.

Listen young children! Hold fast wise aged one!

A tear wakes me, but it is not mine.
I must go, and meet the new day, sharing a love…a dream.

Boy

I once knew a young boy
Who's mind was as vast as the stars
And who's heart was as big as the world.
He often sat in a dark room,
With only the flicker from an old
Worn out candle to light his thoughts.
He wrote of things he had not yet experienced,
and places he had only wished to see.
As he grew, his ambitions became stronger,
And his mind became overwhelmed with greed.
Not of wealth or material,
But of knowledge and intelligence.
His questions became complicated,
And the people to answer them became few.
As time passed he began to realize,
That not all questions were meant to have answers,
And not all of life,
Was meant to be questioned.

Thorn

Through the hallways of my mind,
I discovered a world of similes,
Miniature windows to my soul,
Each peering through a closed blind.

Unable to speak the Biblical truth,
They're umbilically attached to a fear
That refuses to reveal the pain
Caused by indiscretions in my youth.

With the precision of a surgeon's knife,
I exorcised the image of his face,
Stilled the sound of his voice,
And coldly bid adieu to his life.

Yet within the corner of my heart
He lives, the days and nights are one,
And his lifeforce refuses to honor
The alluring weave of time to depart.

Love then, like a thorn in the side,
Refuses to allow the heart to heal,
And manipulates the mind into denial,
Till neither has a place to hide.

Death of a Star

Paling into insignificance, as black turns to white
and white transparent,
from all to nothing in the beat of a heart
and from life to non-existence in the blink of an eye
As ashes to dust, and dust to naught,
the death of a star doth mine mind exalt
Falling from the eternal sky
and spreading it's tears on me, below.
I stare in recognition at the pain and the waste
of such glorious beauty,
From "being", from "existing", to nothing at all
Did an Angel's breath touch my cheek?
As tears of sadness rained upon me
Such miraculous conception as never have I seen
from nothing, does nothing come?
From death is there not birth, or re-birth?
The death of a star, a light extinguished falling, fallen
A silver tail doth trail it to the grave look up,
for as one light dies, another is born.

Destiny

I was bound for destiny,
Though my mind was totally unaware
That I had lived out my fantasy
In the space between here and there;
That time had swept me beyond,
Beyond the Earthly constraints of life
Into a world without a blinking neon,
Or the cutting edge of a desperate knife;
And that I had rejected all I had known,
Freeing myself of knowledge's curse,
Till I was at long last singularly alone
Among the infinite entities of the universe.
I was lost till I was found,
I was nowhere till I was destiny-bound.

Love

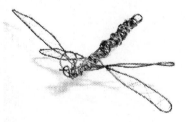

Currents

Infinite time.
Infinite space.
Yet here we are,
The two of us,
Heart to heart
And face to face;
Sharing this one moment,
Sharing this one place.
Sojourners on an endless sea
Coursing through eternity,
Yet I found you
And you found me.

Two quintessential arguments
To silence faith in accidents.

the psalm of love

I thank you Lord
for the love that you have blessed me with
she is gentle
and generous of spirit. kind and loving
and full of life.
I thank you and am humbled by this woman,
who has set me
in her heart and offered to share so much.
amen

wings

If I were to play Daedalus
and fashion you your wings
I would not build from feathers
and bind with wax and strings.

Instead I would seek butterflies
and beg them from my plight
to share with you their chrysalis

so you may, the winds, alight.

For such is your perfection
you need no graver lift
than the scarcest hint of summerwings
to bear Aphrodite's gift.

Unworthy

I have always been what I should be
to brace your strength and set you free
from all your demons and diversions. Weak
am I, clay with flecks of gold. but I seek
to be what you need. accept me back, take
me for all my flaws and failures. this snake
does no more wish to seek to bring you suffering
than you would ask for such a false bartering
of intentions. do not reject me and I will see
your joy as great as it can be made, as my duty.

scrutiny

once.
when you were unaware of my scrutiny.
I watched you cross the room and I
marveled at your form and elegance
as you made poetry of simply motion.
filling my heart with inspiration
that even now, months later, I can
recall with sweet fondness and emotion.

felicific

a vision. a woman, undoubtedly you
by her stance and form and essence.
standing at the window. Watching
a child chasing butterflies across
a field of wildflowers. and smiling
as the afternoon sun warms them
both. and the clouds are always white.

simple pleasure

shall I write poems of passion
that raise the peoples' fire?
shall icons of you I fashion
to stand, idols of desire?
or better should I treasure
every moment that we claim
and seek the simple pleasure
of a common home and name?

ecstasy

the sound of your voice sends echoes across my soul
like the demon-purging rhythms of the kodo drums.
vibrant and intense, these feeling spread the wings
of my twice-born heart and give it the wind. it sings
like the voice of a multitude of angels, the wind comes
and blows away the sand. but it leaves the image whole.

child of love and eloquence

child of love and eloquence. I saw you today, floating
at finger's reach, smiling and cooing. your mother
stands beside me again and we await you. Nothing
gives me greater joy than seeing your approach, nearer
and nearer you draw and I am hopeswept and wrapped
in an enraptured veil of peace and enamorment. I wait
for your arrival, celebrating with a song trapped
from an angel's voice and held immutable at hell's gate.

inevitability

eyes of burnt honey and smile of feral love. Could
I have found anyone, anything to bring me more pleasure?
not merely of the flesh, but of the heart and mind.
you fulfill me and give me back that which I bartered
away a thousand lifetimes ago. I cannot remember
a moment in my life where I do not truly find
you there, or the coming shadow of your inevitability.
and you now are my soulbride, everything to me.

meander

I am phoenix and golem. soulless and reborn.
the son of memory. the father of dreams and fear.
look upon my fruits and know them by their totems.
truth is my iron. love, my tunic. and you, my soul.

Romeo

In the midst of a sea of nameless faces,
For one small moment in time
I was yours and you were mine.
What would you say if I told you
That in that single instant,
you dried my heart's tears
That you silenced the storm in my soul.
In the midst of a sea of nameless faces,
For one small moment in time
I was yours and you were my Romeo.

I Was There

I was there when morning break caressed your lips like fleeting shadows.
I was there when westward winds spoke softly through the trees.
I was there; I said your name, if only in a whisper.
But the tone turned quickly traitor to the tune of billowing breeze.

I had dreamed of dreams as sullen as the sailor lost at sea,
turning starboard to the horizon, spying silhouetted land.
I awoke with you my compass, for now, forsake forever.
I was there, sleeping beside you; I was there, I kissed your hand.

In that hopeful gray haze of haphazard, peaceful slumber;
when the moon descends, the sun awakes, and tomorrow becomes today.
Those brief few morning moments when dark encounters daylight,
even then I had the words and I didn't know what to say.

So when your eyes open to reveal indented, empty pillows.
And you wonder why my words of love, on leaving, are so rare.
Then know that in the morning you are silken, sleeping softly.
And I love you more than ever. That was then and I was there.

Star Fields

You are with me as in a dream.
Your shoulders are the wings that bear us
Everywhere out of this world.
There is no above. There is no beneath.
We ride each color of the prismatic bow.
We are beyond time—past day, past night.
We flit through the rhythm with undaunted accord
Where the music of the spheres is intrepid and bold,
Far from the earth's diaphanous dome,
Far from the cartouche of what is right or appealing.
We weave in and out of each star field
Through which intertwined we soar and race,
Outpacing the metronome of fevered space,
Creating a new kind of living pace.
Our souls together again once more.

Pedestal

Last night,
When you hung up the phone,
I cried.

Then I started to think.
About pedestals.
And what they are.
And who you place on them.

A statue on a pedestal
Is a cold and distant thing.
Beautiful, yes,
But unchanging.

I thought some more.
What is a statue
Next to a good friend?

Statues are to be admired,
Not obsessed over,
A lesson learned from Pygmalion

And I laughed,
Realizing that I can have a friend
And still polish the pedestal.
(Once in a while.)

Gaze of Grace

I've tried on Grace
(flowing body, gentle smile).
It doesn't suit me.
The colors are all wrong.

Naked to the truth, Confidence
(toss a tactful negligee,
slender stride)
made me want to don my robe.

I've long outgrown Beloved's wardrobe
(smiling eyes, head in clouds).
The bulge of reality reflects
a different me.

I've slipped into something comfortable with you
(warm blood, hot breath, soft hands).
In spite of prickly words and restless minds,
you are my favorite slippers, book and music.

You clothe me "beautiful"
and the me I am inside
is warmed by your gaze.

Sketching Inner Landscapes

This morning, as I was walking to the bus stop for the second day of school (only 178 left to go), I saw a man working in his garden. At 6:30 in the morning, in the rain. What was more interesting was that he was happy to be doing it; not peeved that the weeds couldn't wait until the sky was clear or until he came home from work, and not annoyed that his wife made him get up before dawn to tend her petunias. He smiled at me as I passed him, up to his arms in the rich wet loam. The old man was whistling cheerfully, and his crisp, precise notes followed me down the street to where I waited, alone, for a bus that would never come.

Farewell to Reality

When the smallest of dreams
Refuses our wish to come true,
Then listen for the silent screams
Of a heart laden with rue;
Then watch as a life fades
Into the cool, transparent night
Of a world's parlor game charades,
Where the prize is power's might;
Then feel the pain of a lost mind,
Once searching for a way out,
But now spiritless and resigned
To accept what reality's all about.
But if you dream a dream come true,
Bid all of what reality's about adieu.

Blue Foxes

There are blue foxes
in shades of calico.
No child is lonely.
Sullen wolves guard this home.

There are blue foxes—
foxes silent in the night.
A child is not ashamed.
Thirsty wolves live here.

There are blue foxes-
foxes peer through the panes.
A child is not beaten.
Angry wolves howl in this house.

There are blue foxes-
foxes who whisper.
A child is not angry.
Drowning wolves die on this hearth.

There are blue foxes.
They are there.
There is no child.
Furious wolves feed on this heart.

Monstrosity

That which presents itself only dimly
Before the latent eye of the offended
Has untold reservoirs of hiding lairs
Within the wicked, callous hearts of cunning men.

Ever do they rove to and fro upon the earth
Seeking what they may see
Doing that which is unjust and perverse
Storing up ample supplies of corruption
Upon which they may feed in their leaner hours.

Their hearts are old, wizened, dead fruits upon the ground.

Their ears are open to the tawdry, the vile.
Their hands conceal razor-sharp claws of steel,
Perpetually at the ready.

They swagger and sway, head turning to the left, to the right
Seeking whom they may devour.
They prey upon the meek, the simple, the guileless
And the unsuspecting.

Their abode is the birthplace of nightmares.

Eternity

What secrets do your waters hold?
What strange tales could your shores unfold?
Your mountain peaks rise from the sea;
Who can solve their mystery?

Did earth and sea in ages past
Endure one cataclysmic gasp
To make you what you are today?
Or did the hand of God sweep o'er
This vast expanse of space before
The world could say Him nay?

These grains of sand upon your beaches—
Where have they traveled—to what reaches
Beyond our human ken?
To the very depths, to the highest crest,
To give their all, their very best,
Around the world and back again?

Could we perceive God's wondrous plan,
And know the power that rules the sea,
And brings to shore the shifting sands,
We, too, could know eternity.

Tormenter

Tormented by thoughts of doubt,
We dive into the reflection pool
Of life's swirling temptations
With our hands filled with plastic,
The ultimate symbol of our clout.

Tormented by feelings of loneliness,
We surf with today's blend of demos,
Grasping for a morsel of warmth
From an anonymous on line chat,
Or from the personals meant to impress.

Tormented by the noise of the herd,
We seek refuge in a new age,
A crystallized awakening of the soul
Into a world of inner silence,
Till channeled into the absurd.

Facing life with an insatiable reach,
We expose the vulnerable human spirit,
To defeat; if only we would admit
That the true medusan culprit,
Our tentacled tormentor, lies within each.

Treasure

Why as an individual must I fall under
the prey of society's quota. Society demands
that I uphold a certain criteria.

What is the matter with being one's self.
Why can't I perform my tasks and dreams
in the way I see fit?

Does everyone fight so hard for this
treasure that is behind one of life's
arbitrary doors?

Between life and love is one's own
individuality, something I am not allowed
to grasp.

I can only assume it will take until
the end of life's journey to achieve
individuality, that which most could
only dream of:

The treasure behind life's door.

Strings

If everything be superstrings,
is consciousness illusion?
Is science closed to deities'
intolerant intrusion?
If everything be quarks and things,
is 'living', then, a lie?
And this is it, eternally
the same as when I die?

Since all I am is ticky-tacky,
flesh and blood and bone,
then everything is really wacky.
And I feel so alone.
My dreams are only whimperings
with chemicals for hope.
Since all I am is stupid strings,
perhaps I need some rope.

Crossing Over

As we are born, we fall into the light.
Willingly we stay to learn what we must.
As each day, as each year passes,
We are allowed slight glances
As to what we really must learn.

Crossing over.

In our eagerness to gain insight, we rush,
Not truly looking where we must,
We seek the light from which we come,
Not realizing with us it still remains.

Crossing over.

As each day, as each year slips away,
The light comes back to us closer each day.
When we near our goal,
We realize it never left us.

Crossing over.

Our soul is our guide and will always lead
Us back to our Lord, our light.

Crossing over.

Thoughts from Robyn's mother

Every mother watches with awe and wonder as her child grows. We are amazed as this new person reaches out to experience the world around her and we delight in our opportunity to share this wonder and see the world anew through our child's eyes. But often by the time our child reaches her teen years, that door is closed to us and we have very limited access to our child's view of the world. Robyn's writings give us a portal into the mind of a teen confronted with life and her views of the ever-widening world around her. Robyn loved to share her writing with all of us; she sent out emails of her "Poems of the Day" to those she loved, she wrote letters to family and friends, corresponded with fellow lovers of the word on websites, and would spend evenings reading aloud from her works in progress to my husband and me. We watched, amazed as her love for writing and her talent became increasingly more evident.

Yet, nothing prepared us for the quality and volume of her work that we discovered upon her death in October 2000: over 150 poems, hundreds of pages of novels, numerous short stories and essays. All organized (Who ever said she had "organizational dysfunction"?) in files and folders on her laptop and in multiple hardcover journals in her room. That fall, Robyn was enrolled in an advanced placement American History class; her notebook was filled with extensive notes taken in class in a well-organized and thorough outline format. Interspersed within these pages, and obviously written during class while she was listening and taking notes, were approximately twenty pages of a new novel.

As I sat down at her laptop to search for poetry and stories to share with friends and family at her funeral, I was amazed at the number of works I had never seen. In the months that followed, when I had the time to go through and read her work I began to realize what a beautiful gift she had left us. My sister-in-law Gretchen reflected that Robyn's life and writings would leave more of an impact on this world than the lives of many people who live well into adulthood. Writer Russ Cordua included the following dedication to Robyn in his work *Passageways*:

> *Dedicated to the memory of Robyn A. Weiss*
> *1984–2000*
> *Your very existence has brought me clarity.*

When I first read this dedication I had to laugh. Living with Robyn did not bring "clarity" to our lives. Her approach to life was so very different from any I had ever known that we all constantly had to readjust our expectations as we sought to maintain any balance in our lives. It was my husband Ted who often helped me look at life through eyes that accepted Robyn's differences. He explained to me, as we looked over the lawn Robyn had just mowed, that the problem was we were forgetting that a "poet" had cut the grass and we were looking at the final result through the eyes of linear thinkers. Our friend Carolyn Gates listened to me worry that Robyn was not doing her tenth grade school work and then patiently pointed out that Robyn was focusing on her writing and was actually being very productive. And so, I grew in my understanding of my beloved child. I do not know if I would have ever reached a point where I understood Robyn's way of thinking, and I sought that understanding so very desperately. What I have learned since her death, from her words and with the help of friends, family, prayer, and God, is that my understanding of peoples' differences is not what matters. I no longer seek that. Rather, what matters is not a willingness to accept those differences, but a heart open to cherishing the very things that make each of us unique. I do not know if this is the clarity that Russ found in Robyn's work, but it is the most important thing that I learned from the all too brief sixteen years I spent with Robyn.

My wish for you, as you read this book, is that you look back on the times we spent with Robyn with joy, that you remember how she made us laugh and gave her love to us all so freely, and that you too are able to rejoice in the differences you encounter in the people you meet on your journey.

Jacki Edens

Acknowledgements

Acknowledgements

Conversing with Dragons represents the original work and words of Robyn Weiss. However, it also reflects the work, support, and love of many wonderful people. To each of you who encouraged and loved Robyn throughout her life, this book is for you.

At the risk of leaving out someone important, special mention must be made to the following people: Barbara DeCesare and Mimi Zannino-Bracken who, never having met Robyn, took their time to learn about her life and read her work, making the publication of this book possible; Robyn's biggest fan, her beloved grandmother Doris Curreri who helped cull Robyn's many writings down to what you find printed here; the many people who continued to encourage us to publish Robyn's work, especially Aunt Helen, who never spoke to us without asking about the progress of this project; and finally our wonderful editor Linda Joy Burke, whose support of Robyn's art both before and after her death made such a difference in Robyn's life and mine.

JCE

0-595-28743-3